To

GW00457180

MICHELE

XO

LETTERS FROM VERDUN

DIARY and LETTERS

of

AVERY ROYCE WOLFE

Written during his service with

THE AMERICAN FIELD SERVICE

while a member of

SECTION No.31 and SECTION No. 15

June 27, 1917 to April 26, 1919

Letters from VERDUN

Frontline Experiences of an American
Volunteer in World War I France

Compiled and Edited by
WILLIAM C. HARVEY AND ERIC T. HARVEY

CASEMATE
Philadelphia & Newbury

Published in the United States of America and Great Britain in 2009 by
CASEMATE
908 Darby Road, Havertown, PA 19083
and
17 Cheap Street, Newbury RG20 5DD

ISBN 978-1-932033-94-6

Cataloging-in-publication data is available from the Library of Congress
and the British Library.

10 9 8 7 6 5 4 3 2 1

Printed and bound in the United States of America.

For a complete list of Casemate titles please contact:

CASEMATE PUBLISHERS (US)
Telephone (610) 853-9131, Fax (610) 853-9146
E-mail: casemate@casematepublishing.com

CASEMATE PUBLISHERS (UK)
Telephone (01635) 231091, Fax (01635) 41619
E-mail: casemate-uk@casematepublishing.co.uk

Table of Contents

Preface   7

Part I: Summer of 1917   11

Part II: Autumn of 1917   47

Part III: Winter of 1917–1918   95

Part IV: Spring of 1918   145

Pat V: Late Spring and Summer of 1918—The Ludendorff Offensive   193

Epilogue: Final Letters   229

Afterword   236

Glossary of Terms   237

Bibliography and Reference Materials   240

Dedication

In memory of Avery Royce Wolfe,
1898–1977,
a patriot and soldier who left
an enduring legacy of military service.

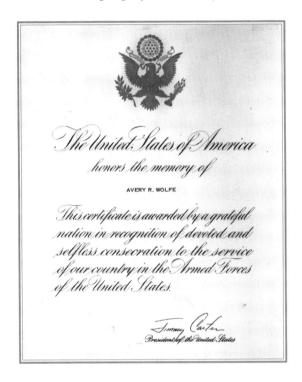

Acknowledgments

Katherine Calabria Harvey generously provided the materials for this volume, and we are equally indebted for her unstinting support and encouragement. We also wish to thank Jane Nearing of the Richardson, Texas, Public Library Research Section for her invaluable assistance, William L. Foley for additional materials from the archives of the William L. Foley Collection, and to Rita P. Harvey for technical assistance.

Preface

Avery Royce Wolfe was born into a middle-class business family on April 30, 1888. He lived in Buffalo, New York, and after his sophomore year at Lafayette College in June 1917, he enlisted as a private in the American Auxiliary Field Service.

In June 1917, 19-year-old Royce Wolfe set out on his "great adventure." He sailed on the French liner *Touraine* from New York City to Bordeaux, and then traveled by train to Paris. He was assigned as an ambulance driver in the American Field Service. He served with the French and then the American Army until his discharge in May 1919.

The American Field Service (AFS) was a volunteer service founded in 1915 by A. Piatt Andrew, an American who wanted to help the French war effort. Under his leadership the organization grew rapidly, often attracting recruits on American college campuses, young men who could establish their "unquestioned loyalty to the allied cause," and who were looking for adventure. Because of the organization's partiality, it was not affiliated with the American Red Cross, which was neutral. Approximately 2,500 volunteers joined the AFS, many long before their country entered the war. One hundred and fifty-one of them lost their lives.

Wolfe entered war service with a number of old friends. Early in his correspondence, he takes pains to explain that he would not go into detail about the actual fighting he witnessed. Rather, he would supply a human narrative of life near the front, in exquisite and often surprising detail, depicting the mortal peril facing ambulance drivers as they toiled in the midst of battle to remove wounded men from the field of fire. The testimonials are accompanied by numerous photographs, most of them his own. Several campaigns are shown in the author's own skillfully drawn maps.

Wolfe's initial idealistic exuberance matured into a sober but unwavering conviction of the rightness of the Allied cause. Later in the war, his passionate hatred of the "Boche" moderated to allow a grudging admiration for German engineering and efficiency, but then the experience of conflict brought him to the realization that enemy and ally share a common humanity.

Wolfe spent his entire war service in the center of the Allied front, within miles of the Verdun sector. He won the coveted French Croix de Guerre for his bravery during the final, desperate Ludendorff offensive of June 1918. Here is a curious gap in this otherwise frequent correspondence; in a letter of early July he apologizes for his neglect, saying only that he had been "very busy."

Wolfe's accounts are competent, detached, and almost clinical—at times poetic and descriptive, and at others more telling in what he doesn't say. His impressions of the soldiers and civilians he meets in foreign parts are an insight into the social and cultural norms of his time. There are touches of dry humor in the poignant homesickness of a young man far from home, pledged to serve for the remainder of the dreadful conflict.

Although the First World War, or Great War, had begun on June 28, 1914, America did not declare war until April 6, 1917, and significant numbers of American troops did not arrive until the summer of 1918. American troops fought in 13 major operations during 200 days of combat, but military tactics had failed to keep pace with military technology, which resulted in a stalemate for much of the war, with enormous casualties sustained on all sides for very little gain. Proportionately more soldiers died of battle wounds than in any war of the previous century. Six men were wounded, taken prisoner, or reported missing for every one killed in battle, but pneumonia still caused more fatalities than combat wounds. In 19 months of campaigning, the American Army suffered 50,000 battle fatalities, 206,000 wounded, and 67,500 deaths due to disease.[1] Five percent of the population living in the U.S. during the First World War served in the armed forces in some way, compared with nearly 12 percent during the Civil War. Two out of every three American soldiers saw action in battle.

The war saw the frightening advent of poison gas as a "weapon of mass destruction," though ironically, the toxic mustard and chlorine gasses were relatively humane weapons. Only 200 men died on the battlefield as a result of acute exposure to poison gas, with 2,200 succumbing in field hospitals, these out of 70,000 total gas casualties among American troops.[2] Wolfe relates that some soldiers deliberately exposed themselves in order to obtain a respite from the battlefield. The vast preponderance of victims experienced acute pulmonary symptoms, and a minority went on to develop severe and disabling chronic lung

---

[1]. Ayres, Leonard P., *The War With Germany—A Statistical Summary* (Washington, DC, 1919), 118.

[2]. Heyman, Neil M., *Daily Life in World War One* (Westport, CT, 2002), 103.

disease. However, the tactical effect on unprotected battlefield troops was devastating, and in 1918, 20–30 percent of all casualties were due to exposure to toxic gases.

Twenty-four million men were registered for induction into the armed forces by the Selective Service Law of May 19, 1917, their ages ranging from 18 to 45. One in eight, or 2,800,000, were inducted, and in the course of America's 19 months of involvement in the war, 2,086,000 Americans were sent overseas, of whom 1,390,000 fought in France.

The division was the main fighting unit of the war and consisted, on average, of 1,000 officers and 27,000 men. Forty-two American divisions were trained and sent to fight overseas, the majority arriving during the last six months of the war and eventually exceeding the British Expeditionary Force in size. Depot Brigades numbering about 10,000 personnel were organized as training and sorting units to process the new men and materials. One in four servicemen was a member of the Services of Supply.

America's involvement in the First World War cost nearly $22,000,000,000, almost as much as it had cost to run the nation between the years 1791 to 1914. This did not include the $10,000,000,000 loaned to the Allies. Two-thirds of the cost of the American war effort went to fund the Army, with expenditures escalating from $2,000,000 per day for the first three months, to $22,000,000 per day for the next year, and finally $44,000,000 per day for the final 10 months. The war cost the Allies and Central Powers an estimated $186,000,000,000, two-thirds of which was expended by the Allied forces, primarily Germany, Great Britain, France, the United States of America, and Austria/Hungary. One-fifth of the cost to the Allied forces was borne by the Americans.

American high explosives and powder were the primary weapons of the Allied war effort for the duration of the conflict. Two million artillery rounds and 3,500,000,000 small arms rounds, of which 1,800,000,000 were shipped overseas, were manufactured for use in the war. Ten thousand tons of gas was produced by the U.S. for the Allies, and by America's entry into the war in 1917, 600,000 Springfield rifles had been manufactured. This was not nearly enough to meet the needs of the Allied and American troops, so the majority of infantrymen were issued the British-designed Enfield rifle, also produced in the U.S. Before the armistice of November 11, 1918, 40,000 trucks were manufactured and shipped to France from the U.S., and 7,500,000 tons of supplies were manufactured in and shipped from the U.S. to France to maintain the war effort.

Part I

Summer of 1917

Introduction

By 1917, only propagandists on either side believed a victory was possible through one final and decisive battle. The worst fears of the earlier visionaries had become manifest. Even commanding generals divulged privately a vision of war that involved all a nation's citizens—men, women, and children—civilian as well as military. This war would destroy entire economies and would not end until the combatants were utterly exhausted.

The grand strategy of a decisive breach of the enemy trench lines, subscribed to by both sides, fell victim on any number of occasions to an inability to exploit significant breakthroughs once they occurred. While the commanders could move men on an unprecedented scale, they lacked the technology to move the requisite food and ammunition to support the offensive. Here we see another instance of theorizing that it would be possible "to punch through the lines, roll up both sides, and end the war." The first part was accomplished on many occasions; the second, never. Having belatedly grasped the tactical advantage of the machine gun and massed artillery, the generals never met the attendant logistical demands.

In the summer of 1917, the line of battle on the Western Front arced north from Switzerland to the English Channel, having changed little from September 1914, the second month of the war. The "war of attrition" went on. Royce Wolfe's ambulance unit was assigned to the French Second Infantry Division (2 DI), which occupied a segment of the front just northwest of the Verdun Salient.

At the beginning of the First World War, the American Ambulance Service operated one hospital in Paris.[3] To house future operations, an expansion was begun on the Lycée Pasteur, a French High School under construction at the time. By 1915, an Inspector General had been appointed to the hospital and the American Field Service was created. In the spring of that year, volunteer American ambulance personnel units were formed in cooperation with the French. By 1916, many such units were operating along the Western

---

[3]. William L Foley [Collection], American Volunteer Ambulance Drivers in World War I: 1914–1918 (Hampden, CT, 2007).

Front. By the time of the federalization of the ambulance services in 1917, 30 ambulance units were in existence, and over 2,500 ambulances and other vehicles were turned over to the French and American armies. The men of these units had also redesigned the structure and features of the ambulances to be used in future service. The Ford truck was the preferred vehicle, as it was reliable and maintenance was straightforward.

Wednesday, June 27th, 1917 – Very hot

After arriving from Crystal Beach on the 8:15, I was met at the Buffalo dock by Father, Mother, and Spencer. Milton was not on hand because he understood I was to leave on Thursday night. Upon arriving home, I completed what little packing I had not finished. While packing John B. called, and after making a few calls to the family, John and I left in his car for the NYC station with the hope of seeing the other boys off. We arrived just too late, so John took me to the Lehigh Valley station. I took leave of the folks, said farewell to John, and boarded the train which left on time.

Thursday, June 28th – Very hot

I had a very good night on the train, which arrived in Easton one and a half hours late. I walked up the hill and saw Mr. Smith, Mrs. Hatch, and a number of the boys and professors who were just finishing up summer school. Later I visited Mrs. Hatch and arranged to have my things sent home. I boarded the 11:30 train and arrived at 23rd St. at 1:30, then went immediately to the Waldorf Hotel and secured Room 43, between Mort Wilkinson and Irv Williams. After arranging my things, I boarded the "L" and went to the office of A.A.F.S. at No. 14. Wall St., received my passport and necessary papers without any difficulty, then went to the French Consul's office and had my passport "visa-d." I then took a surface car up Broadway to 33rd St. and walked to the hotel. No charge is required of men in uniform for riding on cars or subways. While I was taking a bath, Mort and Ed Lowery came in. I had a fine dinner at the Waldorf with Mort, and later walked up 5th to Central Park and back. After writing numerous letters and taking another bath, I retired very much exhausted.

Waldorf Astoria Hotel – June 28th

I arrived in New York this afternoon after stopping in Easton to see Mr. Hatch and getting a few of my things. I received my passport and necessary documents and have been informed that we sail this Saturday afternoon on the *Touraine* of the French Line. I have a room next door to Mort Wilkinson, and Irving Williams shares the adjoining room with Reginald Leper. The hotel has given me a very cheap rate: four dollars a day, which includes three meals and a very comfortable room with a bath.

Tell Milton I am sorry he misunderstood the date of my leaving, and if it wouldn't be too much trouble, please get him some kind of gift for his birthday. Tonight I walked up Fifth Ave. to Central Park with Mort. It is terribly hot here and my uniform is awfully heavy. Promising to write you full particulars of my voyage as soon as possible. I am,

Your loving son

Mort will cable our safe arrival to his mother and she will telephone you. Yes, I have written those letters.

Friday, June 29th – Rain and cooler

Arose at 9:30 very much refreshed, bathed, and had a very good breakfast with Irv and Reg Leper. I took the boys to the passport office to secure their papers, and then returned to the Waldorf for lunch. After lunch I sent to the French Line and obtained my ticket ($87.50), and found out that we were to sail Saturday at 3:00 on the liner *Touraine*.

After visiting Battery Park and the Aquarium, we went to visit Irv's cousin (Mr. Bird 3rd) and obtained from him the use of his house in Paris. We returned to the hotel in time for dinner, later securing tickets for "Oh Boy" at $3 dollars apiece, but it was well worth the price. We returned to the hotel, and after a game of Five Hundred, we retired at about midnight. During the day I had obtained shoes and other required things at Abercrombie, Fitch and Co.

Saturday, June 30th — Cool and fair

I was awakened by a telephone call from Mort who was having trouble obtaining his papers. I got dressed immediately and took a telegram of Mort's down to 14 Wall St. He finally received his papers, and then I took him to the other offices where he received his ticket and had his passport "visa-d." I returned to the hotel and had a hurried lunch, finished packing, and had my baggage taken down. Upon applying for the bill, I found that the Buffalo office had taken all charges over to themselves. Mort and I had our baggage put on a taxi and accompanied it to the dock. I stayed with the baggage and saw that it was inspected and put aboard. Then I had my passport stamped and signed by U.S. authorities on the dock and went aboard. I found my bunk very comfortable. It was a lower in a room with four other bunks. It was also very hot and close, being in an inside stateroom. I immediately began looking around for a more favorable berth and found a very comfortable one for two, which I took possession of after seeing the head purser. Later a chap named Arthpach from Boston moved into the room. I left the cabin after getting settled and went on the deck. It was crowded with mothers and fathers and friends of the boys who were going to sail. After a while, I went on board again and took a deck chair on the starboard side. Three o'clock came and we did not sail. It was very noisy on account of the winches loading the ship. Four and five o'clock passed, and still we had failed to move. At 6:00 the whistle blew, dogs on the nearby wharfs barked, and answering whistles from the tugs made the air quite dizzy with confusion. Hurried goodbyes were said at the command "all aboard," and a general rush for the gangplank ensued.

The hawsers were thrown off, and the boat quietly slipped out of the berth and proceeded down the river. The boys who had been supplied with American flags gathered along the rails and waved a last farewell to the crowds of people on the balcony of the dock. We passed Governor's Island and the Statue of Liberty and entered the Narrows. Upon coming abreast of two U.S. destroyers and a cruiser, we maneuvered into position beside them with our bow pointing up the bay. Our curiosity as to this move was interrupted by a bell announcing dinner. I had previously been assigned to sit at table 51 in the upper dining room, first class. I was very fortunate, as we have the best service in this cabin. The meal was very good. I went on deck again after dinner to find that we were still lying beside the destroyers. It was a wonderful night, cool and clear.

In front of us the mass of lights from New York illuminated the horizon. Quite prominently the Statue of Liberty, illuminated by numerous search lights, stood out against the lights of the city. Newark Bay was studded with the lights of numerous ships lying at anchor, while from the mast-heads of the destroyers, signals were being continuously flashed. Under the spell of this beautiful scene of quiet and restfulness, I gradually fell asleep.

I was awakened shortly by a short blast of a whistle, very close and loud. Jumping up I saw that people were congregating on the port side of the boat, so following the crowd, I made my way to the rails and saw a large tug fastened to the side of the steamer. A gangplank had been lowered, and I noticed at the same time that the deck of the tug was piled with baggage. After the party came aboard, a group of American sailors formed a chain up the plank and moved the baggage aboard. I got into conversation with one of the Jackies and learned that the tug, the *Patrol*, belonged to the Mayor of New York, and that it had been detailed to carry the Italian Mission from Newark to our boat. There was quite a good deal of confusion when this became known on board. As soon as their baggage was aboard, the ship came about and started out to sea. We noticed that the two destroyers were convoying us, so we were very glad that the Italian Mission had come aboard. I retired about 12:30.

Avery Royce Wolfe, from picture taken in Spring 1917.

Sunday, July 1st – Superb weather

This is Milton's birthday. I sent some money home for a little remembrance which I hope he appreciated. I arose about 9:00 after a comfortable rest. I found a bath, but was very much disappointed in it. The water is salty and it is useless to try to use soap, as it does not lather. The best you can do is just immerse yourself long enough to allow the dirt to dissolve off. You feel quite refreshed while in the water, but after drying off you feel sticky and uncomfortable. I found that I was late for breakfast, so I only obtained a few buns and some jam. The bell for dinner rang at 11:00 while I was taking exercise on the deck. The food is very good and tastefully cooked, but I find a good deal of difficulty in ascertaining what the menu is. This afternoon I spent in reading. It appears that no church services are held on French steamers on Sunday, although I have been told that such is not the case on other lines.

The Italian Mission appeared on deck this afternoon. It contains several princes, dukes, etc. If these are a fair example of European nobility, I can understand why the world is gradually turning into one large democracy. The Prince of Undine and his aide are dressed in blue uniforms. They seem to be built like question marks, if not more like shadows. They are always very much in evidence. Supper was at 6:00 again. I must comment on the excellent quality of the food. The evening was wonderful—a large moon illuminated the ship and made the blue surging sea visible for miles around. I was told that the moon was a disadvantage to us, as it makes us more visible to the submarines. I retired about 12:00.

Monday, July 2nd – Fine weather

I forgot to say that the U.S. destroyers left us Sunday night while we were at supper. I missed breakfast again, but dinner is so early that I have decided it best to sleep as late as possible and get up just in time for dinner. The day passed as usual, varying the monotony with a game of bridge and walks around the deck. I have met a number of very nice men and boys. They are congenial, and come from almost every part of the States. As it was very hot last night, I attempted to sleep on deck in my steamer chair, but about 1:00 it commenced to rain. On account of this and the fact that I was not very comfortable, I returned to my bunk and slept very well. I have been talking to a little French marine and he is very interesting. I have been teaching him English, and he has been helping my French. I regret now that I failed to spend more time on my French at school because I find it very useful, if not necessary. A little French woman aboard has volunteered her services to teach the fellows her language. She holds classes every day at 3:00 in the saloon. There are quite a few notables aboard. Mrs. Johnson, wife of Owen Johnson, is the center of activity aboard. She is Italian by birth and has a very wonderful voice. The Italian princes make much of her, as does everyone else. Mr. Sayre, son-in-law of President Wilson, is also aboard. He is going to do Y.M.C.A. work in France. He resembles the President very much. With him is an attractive young girl of about 20 who is going to do hospital work. She is very popular with the young men, as she is the only girl of her type aboard. She seems very sensible and carries herself well. I would like to meet her. Mayor McCormick and wife are also among those on board. The mayor, a very tall and attractive man who in private life is president of the Chicago World, is going to join General Pershing's staff.

Tuesday, July 3rd — Good weather

Missed breakfast again. Arose in time for dinner. The afternoon I devoted to reading. Just before supper there were games on deck in which I participated. They amused the people immensely and were a lot of fun. After supper I played bridge until 11:00, and then went on deck to enjoy the evening. I talked a great while with a young fellow named Connosit, who knew Buffalo and people that lived there.

Wednesday, July 4th — Good weather

The Glorious Fourth. What a novelty it is to be thousands of miles away, surrounded by the solitude and quiet of a great expanse of water, when usually the air is full of the noises of bursting firecrackers and the shrill cries of excited children. It is undoubtedly the most quiet 4th I have ever witnessed, but I can truthfully say that never before have I so appreciated the solemnity of the day.

The simple exercises we held on board were terribly impressive. I awoke in time for lunch which was excellent as usual. At 3:00 all the men in uniform congregated at the bow of the boat and sang the national anthem. After witnessing the raising of the American flag, Mayor McCormick then delivered a brief address in which he impressed upon the boys the greatness and solemnity of the work in which they were about to enter, and also reminded them of the standard which they, as American soldiers, must uphold. Captain de Brosse of the French army, who has been touring the U.S. in quest of horses, was then introduced. In faltering English he paid a tribute to the American people and to those of us who were to join his brothers in the fight for democracy. Later in the afternoon, the passengers met in the *salon de conversation* where we sang the national anthems of the various allied countries and listened to speeches by the Prince of Udine, Mr. Sayre, Mayor McCormick, and Marquis Borsarelli, Under Secretary of State for Italy. Prayer was offered by a French *curé* and we were favored with a few solos by the talented Mrs. Johnson. After a red, white, and blue supper, I played bridge until 2:00 and then retired.

Thursday, July 5th — Misty and cooler

Arose in time for dinner and played cards until supper time. Resumed the game after supper and retired at 1:30. We are now about 1,500 miles from France. We travel about 300 miles a day, which is rather slow in these times of fast steamers. The *Touraine* is about 20 years old, so that explains her tardiness. Things are not as comfortable as they could be, but there is nothing to complain of. We figure to get to Bordeaux about Tuesday, and expect to meet our convoy either Saturday or Sunday. No lights are allowed aboard at night except in the lower cabins and in the card rooms. When the moon is not hidden beneath the clouds, it is quite light on deck.

The boys, or rather a large percentage of them, are doing a lot of gambling. It can be excused because there is so little to do aboard and there is no other way in which to spend money. There is also considerable drinking, but this mainly by young fellows who are not used to this unusual amount of freedom. God knows they will learn their lessons soon enough. I am glad that I have already gone through this unfortunate stage which seems to get to every young fellow. There is a poor "boob" aboard who wears a goatee and mustache, but acts more like a woman than a man. He evidently is an unusual specimen of a spoiled son, for his actions are peculiar indeed. You can readily imagine how a personality of this sort would grate against the nerves of a bunch of good, healthy Americans. Well, to make a long story short, the boys abducted His Highness and forcibly removed his priceless facial decorations. In the tussle the poor fellow's glasses were broken. Afterwards, a few of the older men hunted him up and assured him of their good will. He took the affair gamely.

Friday, July 6th — Cool and clear

I pursued the usual routine of getting up for dinner. The afternoon was interrupted by a meeting of the ambulance men. It was announced that the boys had been divided into three groups, and that Mr. Paxon, who is in charge of the whole unit, would appoint temporary leaders. Ben Shepard was appointed leader of the Buffalo Unit.

Saturday, July 7th – Cool and cloudy

I arose later than usual, just in time for dinner. At a meeting of the men it was announced that we had entered the danger zone, and numerous precautions had to be taken against attack from subs. No lights were to appear on the ship after 6:00. The boats were lashed over the sides and everything was made ready to launch the life boats safely. We had boat drills where everyone was shown his place in the boat. We were told to have our life belts on hand. As the captain of the boat had asked for volunteers to help his men keep watch for subs, the fellows were divided into groups of ten and were on duty two hours a day. I was made corporal of my squad. We were on duty Sunday from 11 to 12 A.M., Monday from 2 to 3 A.M., and 4 to 5 P.M., and Tuesday from 6 to 7. Jack and I succeeded in trimming Jim and Bid very badly today, winning by some 1,200 points.

La Touraine

Sunday, July 8th – Fair and warm

Arose as usual at 11:00 A.M. In the morning, mass was held by a French priest and in the afternoon Protestant services were held in the saloon. The night being wonderful, I decided to sleep on deck. The passengers were all advised to do this to facilitate matters in case we struck a sub. I lay awake a long time, looking at the beautiful sky. The moon was shining very brightly. About 3:15 it started to grow light in the east. The sky was wonderful. My watch on Sunday was uneventful, as were indeed all the watches. We passed very few vessels on the voyage and they were long distances off, probably tramp steamers.

Monday, July 9th – Cool and clear

As I did not get to sleep until late this morning, I slept until 3:00, just in time to get my men on watch, which was uneventful. Played cards after supper until 9:00 and then went on deck. It was extremely dark and a light rain had blown up. I was standing by the rail with Bid, watching the phosphorescent jelly fish in the water when one of the fellows ran up to us and asked us to follow him. When we acquiesced he descended the companionway to the Second Deck. At the bottom of the steps, we found a figure all crumpled up and groaning. We picked him up and carried him to the ship's hospital in the forecastle. In the darkness he had fallen down the companionway, and was only slightly injured. I went to bed about 1:00 and awoke about 4:30. I noticed that the ship had stopped so I hurried up on deck. We had at last sighted land. We could see the light from the lighthouse flash at irregular intervals, and along the horizon stood out a rugged fringe of hills. Off our port side, the pilot ship was pitching in the heavy sea. Soon a little boat came over its side and started for our ship. I went down to the second deck and watched the pilot come aboard. He was a funny, grizzled old man, and he said *"bonjour"* as he stepped aboard and proceeded to the bridge. The captain, who had been on duty for two whole days, was very much relieved. He thanked the boys for helping the watch. During the night we had passed a squadron of French destroyers. I stayed on deck and watched the land grow nearer and nearer. I cannot tell you how glad I was to see land once more. I was not afraid of the Huns, but many of the passengers were. We have certainly had a wonderful voyage. The weather has been calm throughout. We expect to arrive in Bordeaux at about 3:00. It is 60 miles up the river.

21 Rue Raynouard – July 10th

We have arrived safely in Bordeaux this morning after an uneventful voyage. I expect you will learn of my arrival before you receive this letter, as Mort has cabled. I have written a little each day, and am sending you what I have so put down. I hope that you are all well and I assure you that I am well. Write as often as possible and please don't worry about me. I wish you would keep my diary for me, and if possible have it typewritten. Remember me to all my friends. I assure you that I think of you as often as you think of me, so with love to all I am,

      Your loving son.

21 Rue Raynouard, Paris – July 13th

I hope you have received a cable of safe arrival from Bordeaux and also my letters, diary, and postal cards. To continue my diary from the morning that we sighted land, it was a beautiful morning and the view of land, as I undoubtedly told you, was very welcome indeed. After picking up the pilot, we took a winding course through the mouth of the river which is mined. Bordeaux is some 60 miles up the river. We sighted land about 4:30 and we arrived at Bordeaux at about 2:00. It was a very beautiful trip up the river. The scenery was unusual, and very quiet and beautiful. I did not see as much of it as I wanted to because of the necessity of packing and writing. When we arrived at the city, we tied up right behind the *Rochambeau*, which had been burned at the dock just before we came in. The customs officials had come aboard at the mouth of the river and had inspected the baggage and "visa'd" our passports. Upon docking we were divided into groups of five and collected our baggage on deck. We checked it through to Paris, and when everything was arranged, we went ashore and lined up and walked to the *chemin de fer*. We were then told to come back at 9:00 that evening. This left the rest of the afternoon to ourselves, so we went sightseeing about town. It was very quaint and picturesque. We got on the train after a long wait with a lunch composed of hardtack, soda, water, etc. It was a rough journey, believe me—third class—and we didn't get into Paris until 9:00 in the morning. We were met at the train by an A. A. man and were taken in taxis to 21 Rue Raynouard. We were shown our bunks in the barracks and then did innumerable little things. After receiving mess kits, we had dinner that was primitive but good.

The place where we are staying is the old U.S. Consular house, a very beautiful building. It was at one time the home of Benjamin Franklin when he was the first ambassador to France. I met Wells Robinson, a Buffalo lady, who has just returned from Salonica. She is going home July 23rd. I spent the rest of July 11th and 12th in seeing Paris. This city is beyond all my expectations; I never dreamed that such a beautiful place existed. I can't get over it. Some time I will tell you of it. Friday morning the transport boys left at 7:00 for training camp. Practically all the Buffalo boys went with it; I pity them. I have heard some tough stories about that service. I refused to go in it and got an ambulance. The ambulance men leave for camp tomorrow at 4:00 (Saturday). I am writing this on Friday night, just before going to bed to catch a little sleep. I hope you are not worrying about me, and I hope you are all well and that you will get all my letters.

I had my picture taken in uniform today and I will forward it to you. If they get there, give one to Marind. I hope you will write to me as often as possible and ask other people to write, because all the letters don't get over, so the more that are sent, the more I get. I am well and good spirited, so don't worry, please! I will write as often as possible, so don't worry if you don't hear from me for some stretches of time, because letters are liable to get lost. Kiss Spencer for me and remember me to all my friends. '

Your loving son.

Avery Royce Wolfe from picture taken July, 1917 in Paris, France.

May-en-Multien – July 14th

We were called at 4:15 and I got up immediately, did what little packing I had to do, and carried my luggage into the auto park at the bottom of the hill. We were allowed two pieces of baggage and a knapsack. I carried my trunk and made-up a blanket roll of my heavy coat, shoes, etc.

After receiving the usual breakfast of coffee, bread, and milk, we were lined up in the auto park, our baggage was piled into a truck, and then we ourselves were herded into another truck and driven to the railroad station, where we boarded third class cars, and, after a long wait, finally pulled out. After a long, dirty, and tiresome ride we arrived at our destination, a little town about 50 miles from Paris. We are not allowed to mention any names of places or write anything that may be of military importance, as all our letters are censored. We had to unload our own baggage and when this was done, we found that no one had come to meet us, so we walked up to the village inn and had an omelet and glasses of wine. The water is very bad here, so wine is used a lot.

While we were eating, the officer in charge wanted us to go to the camp immediately, but as we had already ordered, he permitted us to stay. After dinner we walked around the town, which is typical of all French towns, and then started to walk to the camp, which is about four miles from the town. A company of artillery (75mm) were resting in the town. We are in the war zone and we see thousands of soldiers and long trains of transports every day. They seem very happy and contented. Although we are 40 miles away from the front lines, we can hear the booming of the guns almost continually, and the ground even trembles slightly. We met an ambulance when we were nearly to the camp, and the boys told us to form into lines and march into camp in columns of two. The camp is located in an old mill. We were assigned beds and set about to make ourselves comfortable. After a very good dinner, I walked to the little town of May-en-Multien. We have to be in bed by 9:30. There are about 80 in the camp, which is in charge of a French lieutenant and an American sub-lieutenant. I went to sleep very tired, indeed. The boys were very sore because they were not allowed to stay in Paris for the 14th, the French National Holiday. It is rumored that there are 80,000 American troops in France. The French are very enthusiastic about the Americans.

May-en-Multien — July 15th — Showers and sunshine

We were called at 6:30 and I got up at the last minute in time for roll call. Some hurried dressing. Then we washed and had breakfast of coffee and milk. The Harvard unit of 25 men left immediately after breakfast. I hear they are going to the Belgian front. I was assigned to fatigue duty for the day and chopped wood all morning. Dinner was very good. Because of my experience in driving Fords, I was put in charge of five men and a car, and I took them out to teach them how to drive. After staying out about three hours, I returned and went on guard from 4–6:00. I am here indefinitely. The camp is a sort of place where the men are sent to learn the French drill and how to drive the Fords. As soon as there are any vacancies in the old sections which are serving at the front, men from this camp are sent up to fill in. Our section number is S.S.U. No. 20.

May-en-Multien lies about 15 miles northeast of the town of Meaux. The railroad station is Crouy-sur-Ourcq. Lieutenant Fisher is in command and here we learned to step to the commands of *"En ligne," "Face à gauche," "Demi-tour à droit,"* and best of all, *"Rompez vos rangs."*

May-en-Multien — July 20th

I have been so busy at camp that I have not had time to write as I would have liked to do, but I will write at length now. I have heard that one of the boats that I think carried some of my mail to you was sunk, so this might be the first you have heard from me. The camp here is very beautiful and comfortable. Bob Wallace and Harry Ramsdell are the only boys who joined the ambulance service from the Buffalo contingent. Harry had some trouble with his eyes and was sent back to Paris. Later he sent Bob a letter saying that he had received an honorable discharge—on account of his eyes—and that he was going back to the States on the 28th of July. I didn't think that he would stay here long. I met some fellows from Rochester here and am having a fine time. The food is very good. We get up at 6:00 and go to bed at 9:30. Most of the boys don't have much to do, but because of my knowledge of Fords, I have been appointed as instructor, and it keeps me pretty busy teaching some of these dummies how to drive. Because I have made myself useful, Sergeant Al Magnus has appointed me to drive the Commissary Lieutenant to Meaux for supplies. It is a pretty drive through hilly country, about 16 kilometers from camp. All the country has been at one time held by the Germans, and old trenches, dug-outs, etc., are very common. Everybody seems to wear a uniform and they are very good looking. Clearly, every woman is in mourning.

The days at the camp are kind of monotonous. We are called at 6:00 and have roll call at 6:30, then breakfast of coffee and bread at 7:00. I would give anything for some good white bread. It is impossible to get it over here. The bread comes in round loaves about eight inches in diameter, and each loaf is marked when it was baked. The bread is issued until it is at least seven days old. At 8:00 we have drill under a French sergeant for two hours. Then from 10–11:15 we have Ford instruction. Dinner is at 11:30, and again we have Ford instruction from 1–4:00. Drill again till 5:00, and then supper at 6:30. Ford instruction is from 7–8:00. Lights out at 9:30. So you see, I have a rather busy day.

The camp is located in an old mill four stories high. The building is in the form of an 'L,' with a stream on one side which turns the old mill wheel and runs the antiquated machinery within the building. The two top floors are devoted to sleeping quarters, and the courtyard below, surrounded with a stone wall and an old iron gate, is furnished with a washroom, dining shack, and parking place for some of the cars.

Section ready to leave.

Paris – July 23rd

Monday the 23rd, Chief Fisher received orders to prepare for a new section. I was asked to pick the men who knew most about the sets. We got orders to leave Thursday at once for Paris. We are a new unit, number 31, and so are to be equipped with new ambulances, which have been donated by the members of the Cotton Exchange of New York. We will probably be the last new section formed, as they are now devoting all their energies to building up the *Camion* Service. We hear that they are getting as many sections as possible in action in preparation for the big drive that the English and French are preparing for the Belgian sector near ??? Everyone seems to think that this is the last kick in the bucket for the Allies. If this fails, I don't know what will happen. Everything conceivable is going to be brought into effect. The Americans are being sent to the Swiss border for training purposes, as far away from the fight as possible.

To continue my story, we reached Paris about12:00 on the 23d and reported immediately to 21 Rue Raynouard. Here we met our *chef*, C. C. Battershell, an old Section 13 man, and our *Sous-chef* Ed Mueller. Our French lieutenant's name is Maillard. We have a happy Irishman by the name of Eugene Flynn as mechanic. Flynn hails from City Island, New York. The majority of the drivers come from Harvard, but there are some from the Midwest and Pennsylvania. They seem to be a good bunch of fellows and we should work together in good shape.

In the afternoon we worked on our cars and checked over our equipment. I had dinner at the club, and later in the evening went out to one of the public baths and had a good cleaning. I got to bed rather early. I arose at 7:00, had breakfast, got a hair-cut, and then worked on the car until dinner. After dinner we had our pictures taken. Later I went to town to do a little shopping. I met Harry Ramsdell and had dinner with him at the Chinese Umbrella. Harry is leaving for the States in about a week. During dinner he showed me a Croix de Guerre medal that he had purchased. I asked him what he had bought it for, and he said that it was a souvenir. I hope he doesn't tell the folks at home that he won it, as Harry has never been anywhere near the front. I arranged for him to take this letter back to the States for me. I am writing this just before going to bed and after hearing our chef talk about our work at the front. My address will continue to be the same. I haven't heard from the States yet, but am expecting to soon. Please don't worry. Remember me to all my friends and tell them to write. I wish you could send me some cigarettes, as the tobacco over here is terrible. Will you please give my love to everyone and let them know I am in fine shape. I will send the picture as soon as I am

American Field Service, Section XXXI at 21 rue Raynouard, Paris.

Érize-la-Petite – August 6th

In case you did not receive it, I will say that I sent you a letter through the courtesy of Harry Ramsdell, who was leaving France about July 28th, explaining my experiences for the last ten days. It is useless for me to write more than once a week because the boats only run every ten days. That one letter will be sufficiently long to let you know what I am doing over here. If it was not for the censorship, I could tell you many interesting experiences. As it is, I suppose my letters are not very interesting. I have now been gone away from home for over a month, and as yet have received no mail. You can imagine how earnestly I want to hear from home. There have been a number of boats sunk of late, so I suppose my mail is at the bottom of the Atlantic.

I see upon observing that only one side of the paper can be used, so I will continue over here. This letter is being written somewhere in the Verdun sector (Érize-la-Petite). We have been stationed in this little town for the last six days. When I said town I should have said, "left of the town," because it has been practically razed to the ground. Only a few sheds and one or two of the smaller buildings are left standing, a result of the German occupation of 1914. I have secured some interesting pictures, which I have hopes of sometime showing you. The people who live here—mostly women and children—live in little sheds, such as those we house chickens and pigs in. They all work very hard, and the result of their labor is shown in the cultivated fields. It is very peculiar to walk through them and see fields of grain separated by long lines of trenches and alleyways of barbed-wire entanglements. The country is fairly covered by this network of trenches and barbed wire. Some of the trenches have fallen in, but most are still intact, and one walking through them finds many interesting relics, such as shells, knives, clothing, etc.

Although the front lines and trenches are 40 miles away, you can hear the rumbling of the artillery fire almost incessantly. This town is on the main road from Verdun to Bar-le-Duc, and an endless line of traffic of all sorts is continually passing. It is the main artery that supplies the hungry mouth of the Verdun salient with fresh men and ammunition. A never-ending line of *camions* rattles down the road, sometimes containing as many as 400 trucks and taking up to three hours to pass a given point. Human fodder, packed in 30 to the truck, their gaunt faces covered with the white, chalky dust drive along in an endless line. Forty-five hundred pass in a single day, for a "grand attack" is to be launched in the near future. They are going to the "attack," so they are privileged to ride in the Annamite-driven "whites." But before returning, after having faced their destiny for their allotted period, they must trudge along on foot, weary—oh so weary—but thankful at least that they have been spared the fate of their comrades who have been left behind.

An endless number of officers' cars adds to the confusion. They go like a shot out of hell, having the right of way over everything else. Add to this the long lines of artillery and their complement of ammunition trains, and you have a faint feeling for this depressing spectacle of man preparing for his own destruction. Even the skies above offer their share towards this gruesome activity, as it is seldom that the roar of fleeting aeroplanes does not add to the general confusion. All these things make one realize what a terrible thing war is.

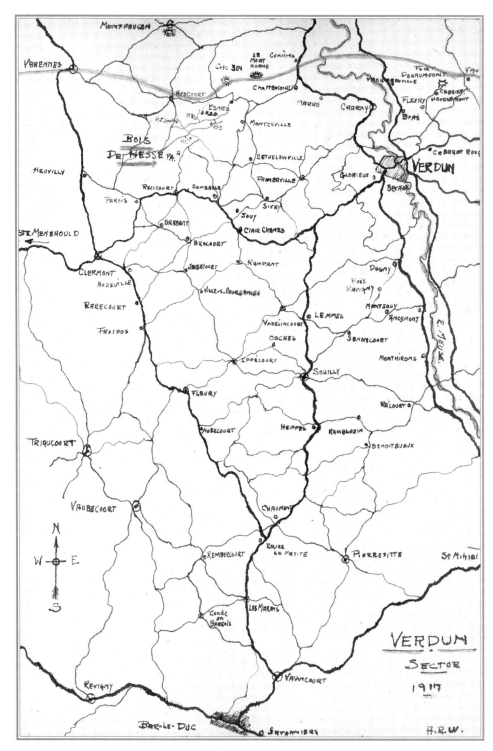

Verdun Sector 1917.

As I said, we have been in this little town now almost ten days, doing nothing but eating and sleeping and taking in the wonderful things that are happening around us. We are patiently waiting to be attached to some army corps so that we can begin our work. Our trip out here from Paris was quite uneventful, with the exception of a few accidents. While still in Paris, one of the fellows ran into the car in front of him and this caused some delay until it was fixed. Here comes in the advantages of a Ford. It took exactly 20 minutes to change the radiator and get the car running again. Everything went along finely until about 5:00 that same afternoon. We travel in convoys, that is to say that some 20 cars in our section follow each other at a distance of about ten yards. Each car has a number, and we can not pass another car or lose our position in the convoy. In our unit we have 20 Ford ambulances, one Ford *camionette*, one white *camion* aid, and an officer's car for the French chef. There are 21 fellows to drive the ambulances and the *camionette*, one American lieutenant, or chef as he is called over here, one American and five French mechanics, two French cooks, a French *Maréchal des Logis*, or supply sergeant, an American *sous-chef*, and the French lieutenant who is in charge. Our chief, Battershell, is a man of about 34 years—a very likable chap. His home is in Milton, Ill. He has been here for over 8 years, coming originally from Section 13. Our French chef, Maillard, is a very nice young Frenchman about 35 years old. He has lived in Chicago three years and therefore speaks English. Although I had no acquaintances in the section before I left Paris, I have come to good terms with all the boys by now, and they are a fine lot. The only trouble is that they are quite young, the average age being 19. Everyone takes me for 23 years old, and believe me, I don't trouble to disillusion them.

To continue our trip from Paris, everything went all right until about 5:00 in the afternoon. Some of the fellows were having trouble with their cars and had to drop out of the convoy. One fellow, Meadowcroft, the chap who came over on the same boat with me and who had his goatee and moustache forcibly removed, pulled a funny one. He had slowed up in attempting to pass a herd of cattle when one of the cows suddenly charged him and caught its horn under the headlight. Before it could be extricated, it had made a hole in the radiator which necessitated a radiator change. Of course the main convoy did not stop for this accident, so the chap who was driving the *camionnette*, Phil Orcutt from Boston, was compelled to tear along in order to catch up with us. Going along pretty fast, he struck a hole and turned completely over. When we went back to find the cause of his delay, we found the *camion* on its side completely wrecked. But Phil, by the grace of God, was unhurt. He had been thrown from the car. Lucky man.

We spent the night in Vitry-le-François, remaining over at this quaint village until Monday morning. After an early start Monday we arrived in Bar-le-Duc before dinner. Bar is the railhead for the Verdun sector. This old, feudal stronghold of the Dukes of Bar lies on the banks of the Ornain, tributary to the River Marne. Famous for its Bar-le-Duc *confiture*, it has now come to be the disembarking place of all those stolid, weary mortals who travel over the "Great White Way" to their destiny of death. In the daytime the town fairly bristles with confused activity, but with the coming of night the town takes on the aspect of a deserted habitation. Not a light shows, and those who are on the move seem furtive in their movements, for the ever-present danger of *Boche* air raids constantly lurks in their thoughts. Can you imagine what it would be like to live under this dreadful uncertainty? Yet the civilians seem happy enough and go about their tasks with the same stolid submissiveness that is so characteristic of the French nation.

American Lieutenant C.C. Battershell and French Lieutenant Maillard, July 1917.

The service maintains a supply depot at Bar, and here we stayed for two days awaiting orders. At Bar I met a chap named Dick Woolworth, whom I knew slightly in Buffalo. He is a lieutenant in the U.S. Army, and is attached to the Second Division which he tells me is in training east of Bar, near the village of Ligny-en Barrois. I also ran across a fellow from Buffalo named Thompson who came over with us, but is now doing Y.M.C.A. work with the American Army. During the first day we were at the Park, two other American ambulances came into town and sat right beside us. You can imagine my surprise to find that George Shearer was attached to one of the sections. We were certainly glad to see each other. He told me that Doc Carr, another Buffalo man, is in his section, but Doc was then in Paris on permission. Isn't it funny how you are bound to meet someone you know wherever you go.

I had another surprising incident. I was talking to Shorty Mills of our section, and he happened to mention that he was connected with a family of Munson. I told him that I, too, had Munson relatives, and then mentioned the story about the ancestor of cousin Sarah, who gave the land upon which Yale University was founded. Shorty was familiar with the story and claimed the same distinction, so we decided that we must be distantly related. Funny, wasn't it?

I really have told you as much as I am allowed to tell about our movements. I am enjoying the best of health, brushing my teeth twice a day, and endeavoring to keep my feet dry, which is quite a task considering the wet weather we have been having. Our food is extremely coarse, but wholesome. How tired I get eating this hard war bread without any butter. I could give anything now for a pan of white bread and butter, a cup of good coffee, and a couple of fried eggs. One never realizes how lucky he is until he is forced into meager conditions. Dad has been such a bountiful provider that I have never realized how fortunate we were. My mouth fairly waters when I think of all the good things you are probably enjoying at home.

There are a few things that I wish I had, despite of the splendid equipment that I had when I came over here. I need a pair of rubber boots, a thermos bottle, and another pair of blankets. In this connection let me tell you a little story about Meadowcroft, the peculiar chap who had the misfortune of losing his facial decorations on the boat. He came in from a trip one cold night to find that Kent Hagler was sick, and had only one blanket. As he was getting ready to turn in, Meadowcroft took two blankets over to Hagler and assured him that he had additional blankets. In the morning I found him lying on the hay with only his overcoat keeping him warm. It's awfully hard to judge a fellow by his looks; I never met a chap who is so absolutely unselfish. I gather from talking to him that he is the only son of a widowed mother. He is a Harvard man who left a position as curator in a department of the Boston Museum to come to France and do his bit. His eyes are very bad and he has to wear thick glasses. How he ever sees driving at night without lights is a mystery to all of us. He is a terrible driver, but somehow he manages to get back. His one fear is being kicked out of the service on account of his eyesight. Lots of other fellows would use that as an excuse to get out of serving in the army entirely. He is much worse than Harry R., who so gallantly fought the battle of Paris before he went home.

Now about cigarettes. I wish that you would send me some, as the French tobacco is vile. There is absolutely nothing else to do but sit around and smoke, so I am sure that you will not begrudge me this pleasure. I would like to have your consent in this matter. I have not heard from any of the boys who went into *Camion*, but the more I hear and see of *Camion* life, the luckier I think I am in joining the Ambulance Service. The story goes the rounds that A. Piatt Andrew received the Legion of Honor from the French for contracting to furnish 5000 American drivers for the transport service. That is the reason for the strenuous effort on behalf of the Paris office to get men to sign up for the *Camion* Service. There is still a great need for ambulance drivers. Well, don't worry about me. Remember me to all my friends who perchance have failed to receive my letters and tell them all to write.

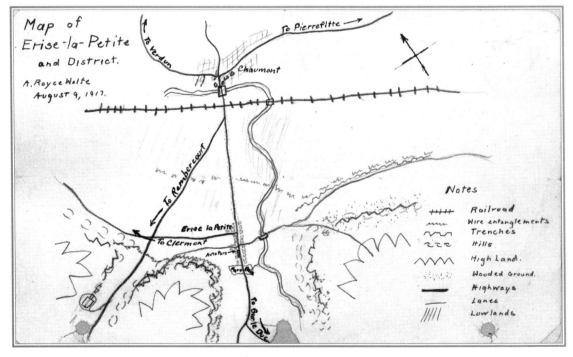

Map of Érize-la-Petite and district.

Érize-la-Petite — August 10th

I am writing this letter tense with excitement and expectation. We have at last been attached to an Army Division, the 25th D.I., and are leaving for the front tomorrow. Leaving at 7:00 in the morning, we are to take over one of the most dangerous sectors on the front. It includes the section to the left of Verdun, immediately in front of the towns of Récicourt and Dombasle. The Bois d'Hesse covers most of the sector, and the Montzeville sector is on the right. The front trenches lie directly in front of the ruined town of Avocourt. We all consider ourselves very fortunate in securing this attachment, as this division is one of the most distinguished in the French army, and the promising and expected dangers will give us a chance to differentiate ourselves. It is not a usual thing for a new section like ours to be offered such a wonderful opportunity. We hope that the French are planning to take the two hills, Le Mort Homme and Côte 304, which lie in front of our sector and a bit to the right. These hills are important, as they command the approaches to Verdun from the right. The Germans have so strongly fortified these hills that the French have concentrated thousands of pieces of artillery, which will put over an intensive barrage lasting three or four days. It is hoped that this preparation will make it easy for the infantry to gain their objective.

Just as we were about to eat supper tonight we witnessed a grand aeroplane duel in the sky. Our attention was called by the bursting of anti-aircraft shells in the air above us. Looking closely, we were able to make out the silver wings of a German plane at quite an altitude. The lone Boche had probably come over the French lines to see where the activities were centered. As we watched the ineffective attempts of the anti-aircraft to scare him away, a squadron of French planes appeared over the skyline to the north, evidently from the aerodrome at Souilly. The Boche did not see them until it was too late, and they were on him like a pack of dogs after a cat. He put up a spectacular fight, getting the first French plane and out-maneuvering the others. But the odds were finally too much for him, and our spectacle ended with the Boche tumbling in flames to the ground, a fiery plummet against the setting sun.

It started to rain this morning, and a cold, chilly drizzle has continued all day. I admit that there is a certain amount of tension in the camp, but I am sure that there is not one of us who does not welcome the opportunity of real action at last. What will the next few days bring to us? Well, I think that I will turn in now and get as much sleep as possible.

Bois de Avocourt, July 1917.

Érize-la-Petite – August 18th

It seems ages since I wrote to you last, when in reality it has been only a few days. In those few days I have passed through the most horrible experiences of my life. We have been initiated into the grim realities of modern warfare. It seems like a fearful nightmare now that we are out of it and recuperating at our little Érize. But our baptism of fire was a great success, and we are now calloused old veterans. Into the last six days have been crowded every single gruesome experience that the war is likely to offer us.

We were such a jubilant bunch of fellows as we pulled out of our cantonment on the morning of August 11th and started for our divisional quarters at Ville-sur-Cousances. We arrived at this little town, some ten miles behind the front at about 10:00, and immediately six of our cars went out to the front to relieve the French section whose duties we were about to take over. The rest of us unloaded the cars and helped make camp. Section 29 was stationed right across the road from us. I knew a number of the fellows whom I was glad to see. They had just lost two of their men and were rather dispirited. Julian Allen had received a piece of *éclat* in the knee, and John Newlin had been hit in the back with another piece. Allen seems to be getting along alright, but Newlin died the night of August fifth at the hospital at Fleury. The accident occurred at the Montzeville *abri*. Although the roads had been thoroughly explained to us before we arrived, we were informed about 6:00 that one of our cars had been lost. The chief was much perturbed and immediately sent out a search party, but without success. Finally, word came that the car was at the triage hospital. It seems that Meadowcroft had taken the wrong turn in leaving P-2, and had almost run into the German lines before he was turned back by an excited and incredulous French officer. He again took another wrong turn and finally landed in Dombasle.

Our French lieutenant was very much annoyed at this episode, and in order to prevent a reoccurrence of this mistake he ordered the section up to Récicourt, much nearer the lines and under continuous shell fire. As there were no other troops in the town, we just picked the least damaged of the few remaining buildings that were standing and proceeded to make ourselves comfortable. We were ordered to sleep in the *abris* which lined the main street. An *abri*, by the way, is a cave covered with sheet iron, sand bags, logs, and earth. Their efficiency lies in their ability to protect humans from flying pieces of shells, called *éclat*, but if the shells should land directly on the *abri*, everything would be blown to pieces.

Abri construction, Post 232.

It was while we were unloading our cars the next morning, August 19, that I heard my first German shell close at hand. I was standing with a small duffle bag in my hands when I heard screech like a sounding claxon horn. Almost immediately I heard the command *couchez* (lie down!), and then a terrific crash, the concussion of which fairly knocked me over. I admit I was practically paralyzed with fright. When I regained my senses and looked about, I saw everyone crouching with their heads to the ground, so I fell as quickly as possible, only just in time, for the fragments of earth, shell, and stone were beginning to fall. Something hit my steel helmet which made me glad I had it on. After a couple of seconds we all got up and looked around. Believe me, it was a pretty scared looking bunch which immediately beat it for the nearest *abri*. We waited in the *abri* until the bombardment was over, and then went out to finish our unpacking. The shell of which I have been speaking landed in the road about 15 feet from us. It was extremely fortunate that none of us was hit. It made a hole some four feet in diameter and about two feet deep in the macadamized road.

I went on duty at 12:00. The road led through a woods all the way. For about a mile and a half it was lined with *abris* and sheds. Great numbers of men and horses were stationed in the woods, out of sight of the enemy's observation balloons and aeroplanes. We passed long trains of ammunition wagons and lines of marching men. At last we pulled up at our objective, P-4, a relay service station serving the heavy artillery. It consisted of a cement *abri*, and a doctor was stationed here with a number of *brancardiers*, or stretcher bearers. We left four cars there and two, including myself, went to post P-2. This is a dressing station about a half a mile behind the trenches. I found that our sector was a very important artillery center. The woods were fairly alive with guns, all cleverly concealed from the enemy. The noise is deafening. At first I would jump every time one went off, but I soon became accustomed to the sound. We were all told to put cotton in our ears to protect our eardrums. A battery of 240 cm. howitzers was stationed not 20 feet from the station's *abri*. It was quite interesting to watch the men work the guns. They fired at the rate of one shot per minute. The shells were about three feet long and a foot in diameter. After a short time, a wounded man was brought in. He was all bloody and was groaning terribly. The doctor bound his wounds up, only stopping the flow of blood as this was just an emergency station. Being seriously wounded, he was sent immediately to the triage hospital in one of our cars. It was so sickening but, like the noise of the shells, one soon gets used to it.

About 3:00 in the afternoon the Boche began to return fire, and we hurriedly retired to the safety of the *abri*. But this proved uninteresting and the air was not at all to my liking, so I cautiously made my way to the entrance, and from that vantage point watched the proceedings. Just as one of the artillery men was entering the *abri*, a shell hit almost in the trench. The concussion flung me back down the stairs. Unhurt, I picked myself up, felt myself all over, and then was pushed to one side by the doctor who rushed up the stairs. Answering his call of assistance, I followed him up to the level. There was the poor artillery man, his head almost completely shot off. With a shrug of his shoulders the doctor motioned for me to assist him. We picked him up, carried him to a hole in the ground, and after the doctor made a record of his name and address from the tag on his arm and removed his personal effects, we let him into the hole and threw a few spadefuls of earth over him. This little episode taught me a very valuable lesson, to wit, never stand near an *abri*

Wire entanglement before Ferme de Moscow.

entrance during a bombardment.

It wasn't long before it was my turn to take wounded and I was told to proceed to Post PJ- Gauche, a *poste de secours* within a few hundred yards of the front trenches. Accompanied by two *brancardiers*, I arrived to find two *couches* awaiting me. The men were terribly mutilated and I immediately started back to the triage at Brocourt. Believe me, that run in itself was some experience. The shells were bursting all around my machine, so naturally, I wanted to go fast, but the poor fellows in the back of my car kept hollering "*doucement.*" And then I had to be continually on the alert to avoid the shell holes in the road. It was a terrible ride, but at last I got to the hospital. One of the fellows had died on the way.

I returned to the relay post at P-4 and tried to get some sleep, but the bursting shells and the foul odors made it impossible. I received my next call at 10:00 in the evening. The night was awfully dark, and of course no lights could be used. Then too, the trees on both sides of the road added to the difficulty of seeing the street. Added to this, I was continually passing long lines of ammunition trucks and other moving vehicles. I don't know yet how I got my car through that night or any subsequent night, but I did, and that is some consolation anyway. I made three trips the night of the twelfth.

I was relieved the next morning and went back to Récicourt to try to get some sleep, but as that was impossible, I went to the pump and was beginning to wash up when the chef came rushing up. One of the fellows' cars had gone *en panne* and he wanted me to take his place. So off I go again and from post P-2, I made three trips that afternoon. I was beginning to get very *fatigué*, as they say over here.

I was relieved again at 6:00 in the evening and again tried to get some sleep, but the fates were against it. It had been 48 hours since I had closed my eyes, and still I was unable to relax because of the thunderous noises from all sides. At 9:00, word came in that the Germans had sprung a gas attack and that two of our cars were unable to pass the mess of horses, carts, and *camions* that obstructed the road at Dead Horse Corner just below. They had taken their cases into an artillery *abri* and had telephoned for instructions. The chief picked three other fellows and myself, and we started out to relieve them. We had proceeded about halfway to post P-2 when some artillery men jumped out into the road and said that it was utterly impossible to get through because of the gas and congestion. But the chief was persistent, so we put on our gasmasks and proceeded. It was a horrible run. Under the masks our breath came in short gasps, like panting dogs. The moisture from our breath covered the lenses of the masks, making it doubly hard to see anything. We shot in and out of traffic that seemed impossible to penetrate. The horses would become suffocated and drop in their tracks.

To add to all this Hell, the Germans started to shell the road. My car was leading the convoy when Bang!, a shell hit a tree at the side of the road which lay fallen across the road, pinning under it a *camion*. That effectively ended our hopes of ever reaching post P-2 that night. Nothing to do but turn around if possible and get out of the filthy gas. In the morning the engineers would unravel the mess of traffic, haul the dead horses to the side of the road, and make it passable. We somehow managed to turn around and started back. It was even more terrible, for by that time we had been in the gas masks for 2 and 1/2 hours, and the masks were only good for three hours. Of necessity I got a few whiffs of the gas. It smells like mustard and burns one's lungs as one inhales it. It was beginning to look pretty desperate when the chief managed to secure a new supply of masks from an artillery *abri*. So we continued on our way, feeling more secure but beginning to feel the effects of the gas. Dead horses and mules lay strewn all over the road. I saw eight of them absolutely blown to smithereens, not ten yards in front of me. They were riding in the back of a *ravitaillement* wagon. Some of the horses we could avoid, but in most cases we had to run over their necks and legs. A shell hit a mule directly in front of me and its anatomy went flying over the landscape and, incidentally, all over my car. At last we reached the fork in the road to Dombasle and the chief told us that we could remove the masks, as we were out of the worst of it. What a relief. The rest of the way to P-4 was simple, but after I had parked my car I began to get dizzy and got quite sick. When I woke up I found myself in the lorry. They told me that I had passed out completely in the best "Desperate Desmond Style."

My throat had a peculiar burning sensation, and when I took a deep breath my chest hurt. The doctor said that I had better call it a day and sent me back to Récicourt. Back at camp I found that two of the cars had been busted up and three of the fellows had gone to the hospital, so there was nothing else to do but go back to work, as the gas cases were to beginning to pile up in an alarming fashion. I didn't do anything that day, but that night (the 13th) I made seven trips. Looking back on it now I don't know how I kept going, for I was really a sick man.

The section had been rolling now for 72 hours without a wink of sleep. We were admittedly pretty well shot up. It had been five days since we had been able to get any rest or good food. Mills and Loomis, the two drivers who had been caught above post P-4, had by this time returned. The section was using an artillery *piste*. We were running again on schedule, but six cars were out of commission, and more than half the section was suffering from the effects of the gas. The peak of the attack had been reached. The French troops had gone over the top on the morning of the 16th and encountered practically no opposition at all. They gained their objective with the loss of only about 50 men. There was less work for us to do than before the attack itself. In spite of the general let down and the fact that we had weathered the storm, our French lieutenant decided to ask that we be relieved.

It was a great disappointment to us, but at the same time we were secretly all very happy when we pulled out of Récicourt the morning of August 18th and headed for good old Érize-la-Petite. We were relieved by Section 17. Meeting one of the boys later, he told me that he had passed the building that we had been cantoned in not two hours after we had left, and that it had been struck by a direct hit and completely demolished. We were lucky.

Back in Érize we are having wonderful weather and as I sit under this tree, looking over fields of ripe grain and orchards heavy with fruit, I can't help but think of those few days as a terrible dream. No one who has not been over here can realize what a dreadful thing this war is. For once I will agree with old Bill Bryan on his "peace at any price" policy. After seeing what I have seen in such a short time, it is wonderful to think the French have stood this thing three long years. It seems terrible to think that there is no way in which to stop this awful war. Believe me, I have already seen enough of this war to last me a lifetime. I really think that I would be quite willing to return to America tomorrow if the opportunity were offered to me.

Artillery men in camp at Érize-la-Petite.

Part 2

Autumn of 1917

Introduction

On the 18th of May 1917, the Selective Service Act was passed into law by Congress in order to meet the demand by the Allies for more men. The Selective Service System eventually registered a total of 24 million men for military service, 23 percent of the total population of the United States at that time. Over four million men would serve in the war as volunteers and conscripts.[4] At the beginning of the war in Europe the United States fielded a Regular Army of 127,588 men, and a National Guard of 181,620, but by the end of 1917, 500,000 draftees and 233,000 volunteers comprised the ranks of the United States Armed Forces as the result of this action.[5]

In mid-April, sporadic mutinies in the French army were occurring and the first troops of the American Expedition Force (AEF) began landing in France. However, no major battle involving American troops would take place until the spring of 1918.

The average American soldier in World War I was trained for six months before sailing for France. There he would receive another two months of training, and serve one month in a quiet sector before being exposed to combat. The division was the main fighting unit of the war, comprising some 1,000 officers and 27,000 men, a ratio of 1 officer to 20 enlisted men. In all, 42 American divisions saw service in World War I.

---

[4]. [National Archives and Records Administration RG163 M1509]

[5]. Ayres, *The War with Germany*, 35

Érize-la-Petite — September 2nd

Dear Aunt Al,

I am supposed to be out on guard duty tonight, but as it is very quiet and disagreeable outside, I have dropped into the barn, our headquarters, to tell you how much I appreciated your letter of the 9th of August, which I received only a few days ago. Our section has just returned from active duty at the front. We evacuated the sector at the extreme left of the last big French drive, which you have probably read about in the papers. The attack itself was a great victory for the French, but it was rather hard on our section. We lost two of our cars from shell fire, and eight of our men are in the hospital suffering from the effects of German gas. The gas produces stomach trouble and a burning sensation in the lungs, both of which are very disagreeable. I myself, being blessed with a robust constitution, have completely recovered from the effects of the gas and am feeling fit and fine.

During the two weeks of the attack, our section carried over 300 wounded from the front lines back to the triage hospitals. A large majority of them were German prisoners, as the casualties suffered by the French were very small due to the excellent preparation for the attack by the artillery. Six thousand French guns of all calibers pounded the German lines for three days and nights before the French troops finally went over the top. The front lines now are to the north of Hills 304 and Le Mort Homme, but the Germans still hold control of the sector by their occupancy of Montfaucon. Although many Germans were captured, many more were needlessly killed due to their stupidity. They had built a system of tunnels in Le Mort Homme, which were very wonderful and an indication of their thoroughness. The main tunnel was about 400 yards long, and lay about 300 feet below the surface from the top of the hill. Here there were three sets of stairs that served as entrances, one at each end and one in the middle. The main tunnel was about 12 feet wide and 7 feet high. It was well timbered and kept dry by a series of pumps. Numerous fans provided a good circulation of air, and these were driven by gasoline powered electrical motors that also furnished electric lights for the entire layout. Off the main passage numerous rooms had been constructed, the largest serving as a hospital and the next largest as officers quarters. These rooms were all nicely furnished with pieces that were probably obtained from the captured French cities. I should judge that the layout would provide very comfortable quarters for several hundred men.

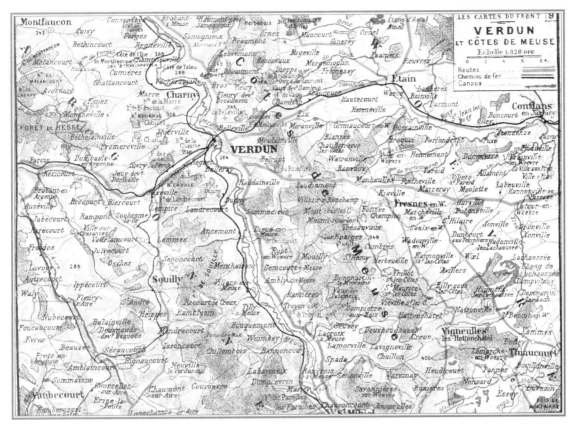

Map of Verdun Sector.

When the French bombardment began, the Germans naturally sought shelter in this perfect retreat. There they were caught napping by the French troops when they finally advanced to the attack. The French called upon them to surrender, and as no reply was forthcoming, they sent an officer down one of the stairways with a white flag. The officer had proceeded about half the way down when the Germans—for some unaccountable reason—started firing, sending the Frenchman tumbling down the stairs. This breach of etiquette so infuriated the French that they plugged up all exits and then shot down quantities of gas and hand grenades. The result was unfortunate, but I suppose that it served the Germans right.

After a few days the French decided that they would like to use the German-made tunnels, so they opened the place up, and after giving it a complete airing, sent men down to check it out. The problem of what to do with all the hundreds of corpses was soon simplified by the decision to stack the corpses like cordwood in one of the larger rooms

Entrance to Tunnel Kronprinz. Sign over entrance in possession of A.R.Wolfe.

opening from the main passage, and then seal up this room very tightly. This was done and the tunnel provided a very good series of quarters. The tunnel, by the way, had been called the "Tunnel *Kronprinz*" by the Germans. I had the good fortune of securing the sign from the main entrance, which I hope to sometime send home with numerous other relics that I have been able to accumulate.

I find it very hard to observe some of the orders that we were given in reference to handling the wounded. We are told that our first duty is to get the wounded back to the hospital as quickly as possible, regardless of whether or not they holler for us to go slowly. It seems that it is imperative to get the wounded to the hospital immediately because their only chance to live depends, many times, on surgical treatment and the sooner that is done, the better the men's chances of living are. So in spite of all their cursing and prayers to go slowly, we plug along through shell-holes and over terrible roads, hoping that the poor souls will survive the trip. When they arrive at the hospital they are immediately given a shot of anti-tetanus in the fleshy part of their legs, and then they are examined by one of the doctors. If an operation is deemed immediately necessary they are taken care of, but if they are only slightly wounded, they are sent to hospitals farther behind the lines for treatment. There are special hospitals for all different cases: gas, contagious diseases, etc., and after a soldier has been confined to a hospital for ten days or more, he is entitled to a leave of absence of one month. Of course, it is needless to say that they all are hoping to receive some slight wound that will enable them to take advantage of this leave of absence.

One night while we were up at the lines I had a series of rather funny experiences. I was sent down with a load consisting of a German *couché*, or lying-down case, and a strapping big negro from the French Colonial Division. The negro was from a division of French Colonials that they had recruited from their colony in Madagascar. They are tremendous specimens, and because they are Mohammedans they make excellent troops, as their religion stipulates that if they are killed facing the enemy, they will immediately go to heaven. So they are absolutely fearless and are among the most efficient French troops. They make up part of the forces that the French call "Storm Troops." They are used solely for the attack, and they are so fearless that they are almost always completely wiped out after every attack that they participate in.

I was going along in pretty good shape, as it was a good night for driving, when I suddenly got a puncture in my left rear wheel. Unluckily, I had stopped just to one side of an ammunition depot near post P-5, and when the Boche started to shell the vicinity just as I had jacked up the car and removed the tire, I can tell you that I was some nervous. In trying to get the new tire on the wheel, one of the tire irons slipped and hit me in the face. The shock knocked me down, but after a few minutes I was able to finish the job and tore out of that area "hell bent for election." I found later that the tire iron had broken one of my front teeth, and that the skin on my nose was broken and bleeding.

I had almost reached the triage hospital at Brocourt when the Boche that I was carrying began to yell so loud that I finally stopped the car and went around to see what it was all about. The German was huddled in one corner, absolutely scared to death. The big negro was sitting on the seat calmly, whetting a huge knife on the sole of his shoe. When I made my appearance he indicated to me that he was going to add a trophy to his necklace. It seems that it is the custom of the Madagascars to cut off the little fingers of their prisoners and wear them on a necklace, as evidence of their fighting ability. A bit shocked and almost as terrified as the poor German, I nevertheless persuaded the negro to wait until

Dead Boche in Le Mort Homme.

we arrived at the hospital so the doctors could witness the fun. Needless to say, when we finally arrived at the hospital the negro was dissuaded from his intention, much to the relief of the German.

It is strange to see how the colored troops are received over in France. There seems to be absolutely no race question, such as exists in America. The negro is accepted everywhere on the same basis as a white men. Even the French girls seem to prefer colored soldiers to white soldiers. I must admit that this is rather repulsive to me, even if I do not have the same prejudice towards the colored people that prevails in our southern states.

As a result of the last attack, the French seem to have revived their spirits. They seem to feel that the Germans have at last lost their *panache*, and that there is a good chance of peace being concluded by the first of the year. Of course, the appearance of American troops has helped their morale immensely, and as a result wherever Americans are in attendance, they are most enthusiastically welcomed. But there is a decided feeling among the soldiers, especially being that America did not come into the war until she had reaped all the advantages of selling the Allies munitions and supplies at outrageous prices, and then felt that she had to get into the scrap herself in order to protect her pocketbook.

We are now *en repos* in what is left of a little village in the north of France, waiting for our men to recuperate before we again go on front-line duty. I said previously that our headquarters was in a barn. I will explain this by saying that this village lay in the path of German destruction in 1914, and everything except this old barn has been razed to the ground. Just outside of this pile of refuse, which once was the home of many a happy peasant, and under the shade of a few remaining apple trees are the graves of women, children, and old men whom the Germans ruthlessly killed. Everywhere you see traces of German ruthlessness. It seems pathetic that France, such a rich and fair county before the war, has now suffered such terrible outrages.

You asked me about the Red Cross work. The Red Cross is doing magnificent work in this war; everywhere you go you see evidence of their valuable efforts. The soldiers are very enthusiastic over their little gifts, which they receive from American women. Writing tablets, cards, tobacco, mufflers, and letters from America are very much in demand, plus a little ready money such as a dollar or two—which is a lot here in France—is very much appreciated. The French soldier gets only five cents a day, and as they are many times not fed very well, there are many little things such as jam, tobacco, etc., which he must buy himself. I have met many soldiers whose rations for four days were a chunk of bread and four small cans of sardines. Nowhere in France, especially in the war zone, is the water fit to drink. This does not work a hardship on the French, as they are used to it, but it is very hard on us Americans who have been brought up on better. We are issued two liters of *pinard*, a cheap red wine, a day. We are supposed to quench our thirsts with this and some very poor coffee that is served in the morning. I did not like the wine at first, but I am gradually getting used to it. Well, I must go out now and look around because the oil in the lamp is getting low. I will be compelled to leave you here with all my love and affection.

Érize-la-Petite – September 7th

I realize that it has been a long time since I have written to you, but you must also consider that I have only heard from you once since I left home. I might have an excuse for not writing, but I don't see why you at home don't take time to write to me, especially as your letters are so very much appreciated.

Homer Gage, Gordon Rogers, and Al Nash.

We are still *en repos* in little old Érize, waiting for something to happen. The fellows have all returned from the hospital and outside of a few trips to Bar-le-Duc, time certainly hangs heavily on our hands. Our French lieutenant and most of the Frenchmen connected to the section have left on permissions. None of us are eligible as yet, but we are all looking forward to the time when we will be able to get back to civilization again. Two of the boys, Schlager and Kent, have left the section and their places have been filled by Gordon Rogers, who hails from Boston and Horace Schenck, who comes from Union, N.Y.

The only news is that our service is to be taken over by the American Army in the very near future. We have been told about it and asked to have our minds made up when the officers come around. We are given to understand that the Service will continue to serve with the French troops, and that everything will remain materially the same, although we will be paid a dollar a day by the Americans and receive the equivalent of 70 cents a day per man for rations. This is quite a windfall in comparison with the 5 cents and 30 cents, respectively, that we are at present receiving from the French. Our obligations with the Field Service will automatically pass when the Army takes us over, so we are at liberty to go home. The enlistment with the Americans is for the duration of the war. Although I would like to come home in some respects, I feel it my duty to stay here, so I shall probably enlist. Perhaps this will meet with your approval; if not, a wire will let me know to the contrary.

As I said before, things are rather dull and quiet here at present. The Germans have taken advantage of the gloriously clear, moonlit nights that we have been enjoying of late to strafe the countryside with almost nightly air raids. They had a nice little party over a large town near here the other night and dropped over 70 bombs, doing much damage and killing several civilians. I happened to be in Bar the next day, so I personally saw the extent of the damage and took some pictures of the shambles. While I was there, about noon, I witnessed a funny scene. I was walking along the street near the station, when all of a sudden the church bells began to ring and sirens began to blow. Every one on the street rushed towards the *caves*, places in the cellars of the homes that are supposed to be bombproof, and the city, which only a few moments before had been alive with commotion and noise, became very quiet and deserted.

We knew what the cause of this sudden evolution was, but as we wished to see for ourselves, we returned out on the street and began to look for the German planes. We located them almost instantly as they were just overhead, two white spots in the sky, surrounded by puffs of white-and-black smoke, anti-aircraft shells exploding in a vain attempt to scare off the invaders. The planes paid no attention to the shells and continued on their way to a point directly over the heart of the city, which only the night before they had bombed so thoroughly. It was an inspiring sight. Every moment we expected to hear a

Children playing near anti-aircraft cave voutée.

bomb fall and burst, so we moved over to the mouth of the *caves* in order to be able to make a quick plunge to safety. To our surprise, the Boche hovered over the city a few minutes and then flew away. As soon as they were out of sight, the city once more resumed its air of business and activity. Everyone seemed to take the incident as a matter of course, and life went along as if nothing had happened. We were told that the Germans had probably returned to take pictures of the damage that their bombs had made the night before. Pretty cold blooded, wasn't it?

I have sent you a little birthday present which I hope you will receive. Best wishes for the day. I made it myself out of some regular cartridges. Ask Milt and Pop to write, and give my best to my friends. Tell Spencer that his big brother hasn't forgotten him. I wish you would send me a fountain pen.

Érize-la-Petite — September 14th

Dear Milt. Well, old man, how are you? I hear from the one letter I have received from home that you are feeling a bit better and playing tennis, golf, and even dancing. Good work old man, but don't overdo it. Well, I expect that by the time you get this letter you will be working hard in school. I suppose you are glad to get back again, especially at your Latin and German. Tell the folks that our section is going out again tomorrow morning. We are going to the little town of Condé-en-Barrois, a little town to the south and west of our present location. There we will join a very famous regiment, the 14th D.I., which is at present *en repos,* but which is scheduled to go to the front in the very near future. All the fellows are back from the hospital and the cars are all in good shape once more. We are all very anxious to see front line service once more.

The other day a friend named Orcutt and I bummed our way on trucks to the aviation field at Souilly. After looking at the planes for some time, we were surprised to hear someone hail us in English. It turned out to be an American attached to the French flying service. He offered to take as up in one of the two-seaters. I took him up and had my first ride in an aeroplane; it surely was a thrill. We went out over the lines and stayed up about 15 minutes.

French pilot ready to start.

Somewhere in France – September 14th

Dear Spencer,

This letter is just for you from your brother, Royce. I hope you are well and have had a good time this summer swimming in the lake and playing in the fields. I wish I could go swimming in the lake again. Where I bathe here, in a brook, the water comes only to my knees and is very cold, so the only time that we go in is when we are in need of a bath.

How are all your little friends? Are you going to Miss Given's school this year, or are you going to go to #66? The boys in the section have acquired two puppies which I wish that you could see. They are just ordinary puppies, but they are very cute indeed and afford us much amusement. We have called one of them Cognac and the other Pinard. I should like very much to bring one of them home with me, and if I do I will give him to you. Goodbye, with love.

Condé-en-Barrois – September 24th

I received your letter of August 29th two days ago. The first letter I received from you came around the middle of August, and I have been receiving mail from you quite regularly since. Evidently, your first letters were lost. I still wish you could write more regularly. I will answer your many questions now to the best of my ability.

The reason why I did not stay with the boys from Buffalo and go into the *Camion* Service is that I had a chance to enter the ambulance service, which the other fellows were not offered, and believe me, I took it. There is no comparison between the two services. The *camions* never go beyond three miles of the front, at least the ones the American boys drive. The work is not interesting in the least, merely carrying ammunition and supplies from the railroad stations to concentration points. Of course, the *camion* service is absolutely safe, but I would rather take a chance once in a while and see some real service and action. I received a letter from one of the fellows yesterday, and he said that the other day he drove his *camion* within three miles of the trenches—he seemed to be elated to think he got so close to the action. Why, we probably saw more action in the few days that we were doing active duty then he will see in all his stay in France. Our work consists of evacuating the front-line trenches, and a lot of our work is done within sight of the German trenches. Now I hope that you will see why I was willing to give up the fellows that I came over here with in order to get into the Ambulance Service. I really think that my decision was for the best, and I know that I am a lot more contented in my present activity.

Your letters are full of news for which I am very thankful. I am glad to hear that Harry Ramsdell was exposed; he certainly was a smooth one. Imagine trying to get easy with that hero stuff when he was never more than 20 miles from Paris at any time. And wasn't it funny that he should have shown that Croix de Guerre to everyone and claimed that he was awarded it for bravery. I think I told you that he showed me that medal while we were having dinner the night before I left for the front. I am glad that you received my pictures and that you liked them. I am sending another today taken with my Ford as we left Paris. I also have a lot of camera pictures which will soon be forthcoming. I got a letter from Aunt Grace the other day, blessing me and asking for something from Paris.

We have been in this little town now since September 15th, waiting for our division, the 14th D. I., to get orders to go to the front once again. Our division is a very

Avery Royce Wolfe as he left Paris on July 12th, 1917.

distinguished attacking division. All the regiments have been cited at least three times, and so the men are all entitled to wear the Croix de Guerre cord around their shoulders, and they are very proud of them. They only lost about a quarter of their men in the last attack, so they are considering themselves very lucky. I must explain that an attacking division is one that goes over the top and occupies the German trenches. When they have solidified their position and everything is quiet once more, they are moved back into the interior and holding divisions, composed of the older men, and hold the position which the younger men have taken. When the attacking division goes *en repos,* they rest and train new men to fill up the ranks of those whom they have lost—as in killed and wounded during the previous attack. When they are again ready for the attack, they go cheerfully along, knowing fully that half of them, under normal circumstances, will fail to come back. Such is war.

American soldiers are getting to be a common sight over here now. They are gradually taking over the supervision and operation of the railroads, and the soldiers are going through intensive training so that they will soon be able to take over some of the French front. They don't seem very anxious to get into action, and believe me, they will be less anxious after they have served a while in the trenches. Nobody can realize how terrible it is until they have actually experienced it. I am afraid that the people in the States don't realize what a terrible mess they have stuck their boot into. But wait until the first list of Americans killed and wounded reaches them. Then they will awake and begin to hate the Germans as we all have learned to do over here.

Over here we don't get nearly as much news as you do about the war, but it seems to be the general opinion that if the president runs things right, this war can't last another year. We are all hoping to see the president issue a proclamation compelling all neutral nations to take sides with the Allies if they wish to get American supplies. This would stop the leakage of ammunition and supplies into Germany, and do a lot in hastening the end of the war. From all indications, the Germans seem to have lost their punch. This means that they have reached a stage where all their energies have got to be devoted to sustaining their hold on their present positions. If sufficient pressure can be brought to bear on all fronts, the Germans would be compelled to give up ground and prisoners, and they would certainly lose a good number of their men. The more men they lose, the weaker they become because their supply is limited. The Germans have complete control of the air, which is a great consideration to their advantage. Since the French lost two of their most famous pilots recently, their air service has become almost completely demoralized, and I understand that the British Air Service is not much better. It all comes from the knowledge that the Germans have, admittedly, faster and better planes, and a fight in the air under these conditions is hardly a sporting affair. Well, we can all have our theories about the war, but the most we can do is our part and pray for the end.

Well, I haven't much more news for you, and my letters are bound to be further uninteresting because of the censorship. I hope that you are all well and enjoying life. The only thing I wish for is tobacco; it is really a necessity. I can endure almost anything if I have a pipe or a cigarette. Tell Wilt I received his letter and the pictures, and I shall write him soon. Hope Dad has plenty of business, but not so much that he will have to work too hard. I have written to everyone and hope they will write to me. Don't you like my moustache? It really is getting to be quite a bush by now. I am thinking seriously of growing a beard as it is quite the fashion over here.

Well, almost forgot to tell you the most important bit of news. The American Army recruiting officers came around on the 27th, and I signed up for the rest of the war. They arrived late one afternoon, just in time for supper. They gave us quite a talk, telling us that we were free agents and that we could make our own decisions. They explained that the service would remain materially the same, and that in all probability we would continue to serve with the French. They said that we would receive American pay and ration money. After supper, those of us that had decided to join received a physical examination, and then when we had passed this, signed on the dotted line. So, your son is in the Army now for the duration of the war and I hope that this meets with your approval. Most of the fellows joined, McGrath and Orcutt being the only two who decided to go home. Ed Mueller, who had been over since the first of the year, decided to take a leave of absence since he had been away from home for such a long time. They appointed Doug Woolley as *sous-chef* in Mueller's place, so Doug will now rate as a first sergeant.

Main St., Condé-en-Barrios.

Little Condé-en-Barrois – October 3rd

Dear Folks,

This letter to you finds us still *en repos* at this quaint little village. We are naturally anxious to get back into front line service, but there have been so many activities of late that we are enjoying ourselves thoroughly. I think that I have told you about the concert that the division gave, and also the soccer game between the soldiers of the 14th D.I. and our section. As a result of our participation in these activities, we have come to very friendly terms with the officers and men of the 14th, and many of the boys have been entertained by the officers. I had lunch with the colonel of the 14th the other day, and had a grand meal and a very interesting time. Shorty Mills came along with me, and we were both amused at the utter lack of information the French have about America. They asked the most amusing questions, even stating that it must be very dangerous to live in the west, on account of the Indians. Their picture of America has evidently been derived from the American movies depicting the Old Wild West.

I had an interesting experience last night. I was on call at the Medicine Chef's when it was decided to send one of the officers that had been recuperating with the regiment to Bar-le-Duc, so that he would be able to catch the Paris train which left Bar that night at 12:00. It was a great night, and the drive was very easy because of a large moon. As we approached Bar, however, we noticed that it was receiving one of its regular visits from the Boche planes, so we drove rather slowly, hoping that they would have dropped their calling cards and departed before we got into the town. Everything went well until we were about to enter the Place de la Gare, where the H.O.E. was located. As I drove up to the entrance of the station, I noticed that everything seemed unusually deserted, and so it was with some idea of what was happening that I quickly ran into the building and hollered for some one to help carry the officer into the room. As I hollered and looked about frantically, a tremendous detonation almost threw me to the floor. Running out, I saw that a bomb had landed in the Square, right around the front of the hotel. Thoroughly frightened by now, I was jolted into action by the arrival of another bomb, which landed in the railroad yard just beyond the station. The officer was yelling to me to take him out of the danger, and so after one last look in the H.O.E., I decided to get into my car and beat a hasty retreat to a spot less liable to attract the German fire. I drove like mad until I hit some large trees on the

Bar-le-Duc on the morning of October 4, 1917.

outskirts of the town, and there waited for the trouble to blow over. We were fairly safe here, so I had plenty of time to gather together my scattered wits, and as I looked back over the town, I noticed that a large fire had started in the business section near the main square.

Soon the anti-air guns quieted down and I felt reasonably sure that the Boche had finished for the night. So I cranked up the old bus and headed into town. The fire by this time was quite serious, and the fire department, with their antiquated equipment and the men themselves wearing their funny steel and brass helmets, were doing their best to prevent the fire from spreading. I got rid of my officer patient and found that the attendants had all taken to the safety of the *abris* at the first indication of the Boche in the sky. They told me that I was crazy to approach the railroad station, as that was always the objective of the German raids. I learned my lesson and will know what not to do in the future. Turning back to Condé, I watched the efforts of the firemen for awhile and took a picture of the fire, which I do not believe will turn out. The trip back was uneventful, and I had a good story to tell the boys the next morning.

Shorty and I have found a little drinking place in town where we can get the best omelet. The store is run by a little old lady and her daughter, Susanne. She is very pretty, so it is a double pleasure that we enjoy when we go up there each night for our omelet and bottle of wine. We have not told the fellows about our find, and hope that we can keep it a secret, as we would otherwise have lots of competition.

Our French mechanic is a jolly soul. He is a young chap from the south named Ojéy. He enlisted in 1914 when he was only 18 years old and has been active ever since. He received a bad wound near the end of his spinal column, which has refused to heal and has to be treated continuously. He has a little dog named Bobby who is the pet of the section. Our *maréchal de logis* is a chap named L'Aborderie, a pompous little fellow with whom we get along quite well, although he does get under our skin occasionally. The driver of the French lieutenant's car is a fellow named François, a nice chap who is very quiet and reserved. In fact, we like all the French who are attached to our section with the one exception of the chef, François. For some unknown reason, he has taken a dislike to us, and we have not been long in realizing it. It may be due to the fact that we do not like the greasy way in which he cooks his food. We have tried to tell him how to cook so that it will be more appetizing to us, but he always goes into a fury and refuses to cooperate in any way. It has gotten to be so bad that we have asked the lieutenant to have him transferred.

Well, this has been a longer letter than I had intended to write, but I hope that it has not bored you to death.

Our Maréchal de Logis, L'Aborderie.

Chef François and Mechanic Ojéy with Bobby in Jouy, 1917.

Condé-en-Barrois – October 4th

I haven't heard from you in some time, but I hope you have received my letters. We are leaving for the front again tomorrow, so I thought I would drop you a line now, as I may be too busy to write when we get working. We are going take over a sector to the immediate right of the division that we worked when we were last up in September. We will be cantoned in the little village of Jouy-en-Argonne. Our posts will start at Montzeville, and then we will have runs from here to Esnes and Posts # 232 and # 239. Our triage hospital will be at Rampont, and there will be a few cars on duty for evacuation work as long as the sector remains quiet.

We have certainly enjoyed our stay in Condé. The weather has been good and things have been quite lively. The soldiers gave a concert last Sunday at which I played my mandolin, and one of the boys sang some American ragtime songs and did an Hawaiian dance. The soldiers were all very pleased. Last Monday we played soccer football with a picked team from our division and they beat us four to nothing. It was very exciting, and the large crowd of onlookers enjoyed it very much, although I must admit that they were a bit partisan. We all found that we were sadly out of condition, and we were a pretty near-winded bunch when the game finally came to an end. Wednesday we were invited to attend a concert given be some real actors who are traveling along the front entertaining the soldiers. It proved to be very good. To our surprise an American opera singer, Miss Nina May, was among the singers. We all met her after the performance. It seemed very good to meet an American woman again. I am sending on the program which I hope that you will keep for me.

Main Street at Montzeville.

The Germans bombed Bar-le-Duc last night and did more damage. If they keep it up, there won't be much left of the town. One of the boys received some American cigarettes today, and we are all enjoying our first good smoke in many a day. French tobacco is terrible, so I do hope you will send me some cigarettes soon. Murads preferred, but I am not particular. Send around 1000 of them in small packages of about 100. In this may they might come through unmolested.

We were able to buy some white flour the other day and one of the fellows, Bond, made an apple pie. Gee it was good! It made us all wish we were home again. It has been very pleasant here in Conde, but we all welcome the opportunity of again seeing active service. Orcutt, McGrath, and Mueller have left, and their places have been filled with three new men: Fred S. Muhlhauser of New Brunswick, N.J., Louis Schneider of Newark, N.J., and ???

Condé soccer game, 14 D.I.-5, S.S.U.31—1. Left to Right: Bingham, Loomis, Kielty, Flynn, Wolfe, Rogers

Jouy-en-Argonne – October 9th

Dear Dad,

I am sure that I have mentioned in one of my previous letters that I have been moved up to the front again, and am engaged in active work. We have been very busy getting acquainted with our new posts and ironing out the routine. Once things are organized, we are able to work along smoothly, and unless interrupted by an attack, life is really quite monotonous. In this connection, it might be of interest to you to learn how our service is organized. The French system differs in all respects from the American in that all motorized transportation is grouped together under one head, the Service of Automobiles. Any demand for motor equipment, whether it be for troop, ammunition, or wounded transportation, must be made to this service, which has complete responsibility for the autos, plus the management and training of the drivers. In regard to ambulances, each division on active duty at the front is allotted a unit composed of 20 cars, and the personnel necessary to drive the them and keep them in condition.

The duty of these cars is the quick transportation of the wounded from the front line dressing stations to the field hospitals. From the field hospitals, another branch of the service, using larger and heavier cars, takes the wounded to various specialty hospitals or to the H.O.E., as the case may be.

A division of the French army is usually composed of three regiments of infantry and a regiment of artillery. Each regiment has its own complement of doctors and stretcher-bearers. In addition, each division has a separate corps of doctors and *brancardiers*, or G.B.D. as they are called, that maintains at least one dressing station, or *poste de secours*, where re-examinations are made and further treatment is given when necessary, and acts as reserve for the regimental first aid units. The G.B.D. also maintains a divisional clearing house, or assortment hospital—the triage— through which all divisional casualties must be cleared and assigned to the various specialty hospitals in the rear, which are under the supervision of the army, or *Corps d'Armée*.

Therefore a man being badly wounded, say as a result of a shell fragment piercing his leg, will be carried by his comrades, or regimental *brancardiers*, to the dressing station where he will receive an examination by the doctor, his wounds will be dressed, and he then will be carried back to the G.B.D. *post de secours* by the regimental *brancardiers*.

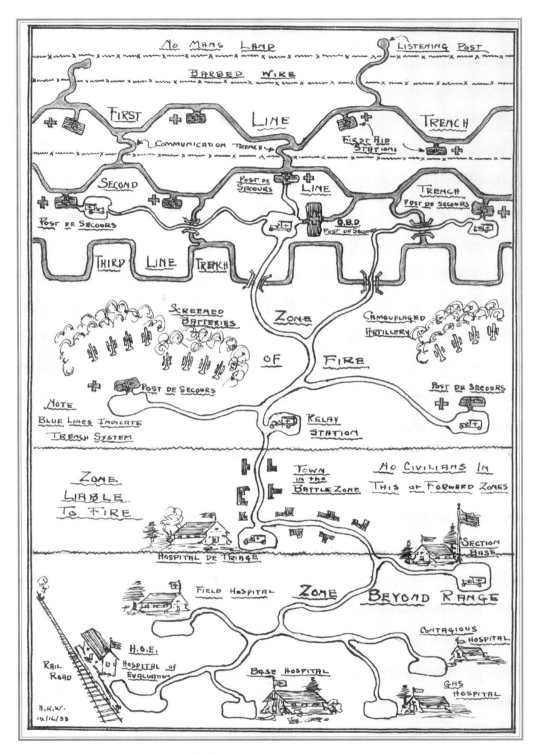

Field Service organization chart.

Once at the G.B.D. post, he will be re-examined, his wound redressed if necessary, and then he will be given a tag, upon which his name and regiment will be recorded, along with comments by the doctor as to the nature of the wound. Different colored tags denote specific cases, such as a yellow tag for gas cases, a red tag for gravely wounded, etc. The man is then placed in one of our cars and transported to the triage hospital, a distance varying with the nature of the front— sometimes three miles, sometimes ten. Here the man is received and immediately given a shot of anti-tetanus in the fleshy part of his leg. He undergoes another examination if necessary, and is later sent back to one of the specialty hospitals, or taken to some railhead for transportation back into the interior. In quiet times, our work is usually laid out on the following plan. Our cars are divided into four or five squads with each one working for 48 hours. The cars then proceed to the front, one car dropping off at the relay station which is on the direct road from the front to the triage hospital. The others proceed, one going to the *poste de secours* of the artillery regiment, one going to the G.B.D. *poste de secours*, and the others going to the regimental *poste de secours*, that is, if the roads are at all passable.

In case it is impossible to reach the regimental posts, all three cars are held at the G.B.D. post and operate from there. When a load has been received at either the regimental or G.B.D. post, the driver proceeds to the triage, stopping at the relay station on the way down and waking up the driver posted there. This driver then takes his car to the post that the other driver has just left. After reaching the triage, the driver returns to the relay station, and he sits and waits for the next car to come down.

Montzeville from the road to Post 239.

In the winter, or when things are unusually slow, the section reduces the number of cars at the front and designates two cars to do the evacuation work, which is the transportation of the cars from the triage to the H.O.E., the base hospital, or the various specialty hospitals. In case of a grand attack the whole division works continuously, adding additional G.B.D. and regimental posts and the rest of the cars being held at the relay station. In such cases, the mortality among the *brancardiers* is so great, that the drivers themselves are compelled to assist the regimental units in getting the wounded from the front to the cars. Carrying a wounded man on a stretcher through a barrage is one of the surest ways of kissing yourself goodbye. When a shell approaches, you can't very well let the poor fellow drop, so you keep plugging away and hope for the best.

Jouy-en-Argonne – October 25th

This letter will be posted in the States by Ed Mueller, a member of our section who is returning there. I will therefore be able to write to you without fear of the censor.

Our section is attached to the 14th Division of Infantry, which is part of the French Second Army that has command of the Verdun Sector. The division is one of "aces," that is to say that each of the four regiments of infantry, and the regiment of artillery comprising their division, has been cited in the orders of the day at least three times, and they all wear the *fouragèrre*. It is the only division of its kind and is the pride of France.

Our division is holding the sector at the immediate left of Verdun, containing such famous battlegrounds as Le Mort Homme, Côte 304, Montzeville, Esnes, Bethinville; all of which have been mentioned time after time in the papers. If you look on the map, you will find them very easily. We are cantoned at Jouy-en-Argonne, a little town near Rampont.

Our 20 cars are divided into four squads of five cars each, and every four days one of the squads is on duty. The cars leave at 1:00 in the afternoon. Two go to Montzeville, which is at present about a mile back of the line, and the other two cars go to the triage hospital at Rampont. From Montzeville one of the cars goes to Post 239, a receiving station where the captain of doctors and stretcher-bearers directs his work. This post is merely a fair *abri*, and as it is in sight of the German lines, we have to back our cars into a crevice

Headquarters at Jouy.

between two mounds of earth and cover them with green canvas so that they cannot be seen. We wait here until the stretcher-bearers bring in enough wounded, and then we run back to the hospital at Rampont. Afterwards we then return to Montzeville, the car there having gone up to Post 239 as we passed on the way down. As soon as it gets dark at about 4:30, the car at Post 239 goes to Post 232, a dressing station in the last line of trenches. We work from here until daybreak, and then return to 239. We are compelled to work Post 232 in the dark because the Germans can see the whole road from 239 to 232, so traffic is forbidden in the daytime. The run from 232 to the hospital at Rampont in the night is our hardest piece of work.

The boys who get hospital work to do have it fairly easy. The *hôpital de triage* is merely a sorting place where the wounded and sick are assessed. Our work here is to carry the wounded to the different hospitals. One of the hospitals is at Fleury, where a regiment of Americans and engineers are stationed. Although they are in no danger, have fine barracks and good American food, they are discontented and anxious to get home.

Americans are getting to be a fairly common sight over here now. They will probably go into the trenches next spring. The French, who are about all in, await their coming very anxiously. If the Americans had not entered, the war would be over now. The French admit they are beaten and they all say that if we had not declared war, they would have made a separate peace. Things are very bad over here. On account of the cold weather coming on,

French priest and my guide on trip to Le Mort Homme in Jouy, 1917.

the fighting has slackened somewhat. Soon winter will force both sides to suspend fighting to any great extent. We all hope that our division will go back *en repos* soon, so that we will be able to get better quarters. We are sleeping in an old hayloft with half the roof shot away. It rains incessantly and it is very cold and wet most of the time. War is passable in summer, but in winter it is rotten. I was talking to one of the French doctors the other day and he told me that there was outright mutiny in several of the French divisions this summer. The situation was so serious that the divisions had to be broken up and dispersed into various parts of the interior.

I took a walk up to Le Mort Homme with a French priest the other day. I entered the famous tunnels that run under this old German fortification and saw many gruesome sights. The French have not had time to clear out the place completely, and one is greeted with half-decayed Germans on every side. We got out of there very quickly because of the smell, and then winded our way through the communication trenches until we reached the first line trench. I was very much surprised at what I saw. I expected to see a lot of men standing in water up to their knees, but there were only sentinels posted every 50 feet or so. The men were in *abris* and all seemed a trifle strained, but contented nevertheless. I never saw a man so looked up to as was the priest; he was a great favorite with the men. At last we came to a little cleared space dug in the side of the hill where three bundles lay next to a hole in the ground. The little group of men that surrounded the spot gave way as the priest approached. He pulled out his prayer book, crossed himself and read from the book. The bundles were then let down into the hole and covered with earth. They had been hit with a shell the day before. On our trip up and back, the priest was being continually stopped by some individual who wished the priest to bless some good luck charm that all the soldiers seem to wear. They all seem to be very superstitious and religious. I have never as yet run across a Protestant minister.

I received your letter of October the 2nd today which came along in very good time. Glad that you received the knife. Ed Mueller may drop in to see you on his trip west and if he does, please see that he has a good time. As there is a possibility of going on a permission in the near future, I wish that you would forward me some money via the American Express.

Jouy-en-Argonne — October 28th

Dear Marion,

Your letter of October 7th came in today, having made a very quick passage indeed. I was very pleased to hear from you, because I was beginning to fear that you had received none of my letters. It must be really pleasant at Wellesley for you with Keller and Elsa there, too. Tell Keller that I thought she would decide to go to Wellesley after all her indecision. I was also mighty pleased to hear what you said about John. There is not another fellow I know who has more ability and promise than John. All he needs is good, sound advice and someone to work for. You have done wonders for him so far, and I think that he knows and appreciates what you have accomplished. That mysterious letter to John that you spoke about, it seems that I made a mistake in the address and those foolish, unthinking postal authorities sent it all the way back to me. The most stupid thing I ever heard of. That box of good cheer that you and Elsa forwarded to me will be looked forward to with the greatest amount of anticipation.

I think it would interest you if I attempted to paint a picture of the place where I am writing this letter. Try to imagine yourself for a moment in a stretch of the dreariest, most desolate land in the whole world. Before you, out of the virtual sea of wet, sticky mud, arise

Path leading to Mort Homme from Post 232, 1917.

two huge mounds of shell-pitted earth. These are two famous hills that have been robbed of every bit of vegetation by the scourge of war. Look to your right and left and all you see is mud. Back yonder, away in the distance, arises another range of hills. These hills are the proud possessors of a fringe of trees which stands out like weird shapes against the quickly disappearing twilight. Extract your feet as best you can from the sticky mud and plod up the resemblance of a road which winds itself through the mud, partially sheltered from German eyes by a low promontory. To your left is a long row of huts built into the ground, about whose doors are loafing a few mud-bespattered *poilus*, who greet you with a "*Ça va, camarade American.*" Finally we come to the last hut, and turning on your electric torch—which you always have at hand—you open the flimsy door and to your surprise, you begin to descend a series of steps dug out of the hard earth. The passage is dark, damp, and full of smoke, so you are thankful when you take your 45th step which brings you into a little room about 12 feet long by 8 feet wide and 7 feet high. This is the *abri* which will be your home for the night. In one corner, sitting before a tiny table overloaded with papers and writing equipment, sits a cheery little French doctor who greets you with a hearty cry and does everything in his power to make you comfortable. In another corner is a small wood stove which furnishes the heat and, incidentally, the smoke for this princely compartment. Over the doctor's desk is a large case containing surgical instruments. All the rest of the small space is mostly taken up by piled rolls of bandages and first aid equipment. You sit down on one of the benches that adorn the room, and after trying vainly for almost an hour to make the doctor understand your best grade of French, and you his best grade of English, you give up in despair and move over near the stove, where if you are at all fatigued— as you generally are— you drop off into a doze. No doubt you will be awakened presently by a shuffling of feet on the stairs. It is two stretcher-bearers carrying between them the limp form of a man. A hand grenade had gone off in front of him and tore a nasty wound in his side. You shake the doctor and then hang around listlessly, sometimes giving the doctor a hand until he has swabbed out and bandaged the wound. If it is very dangerous, you take the poor fellow back to the triage hospital immediately, some eight or ten miles behind the lines, in your little old Ford. If not a dangerous wound, you wait until you get a full load of either five *assis* or three *couches*. When it gets light enough to see clearly, if you have no wounded to take back to the hospitals, you must leave this post and drive back to the next post further behind the lines because no traffic is allowed over this road in the daytime, as the Boche can see it readily, and they are only too willing to take a potshot at you if you make yourself apparent.

Post at Hill 232.

If you can picture to yourself what I have written, you will get a good idea of our work when things are quiet. Of course in times of an attack, everything is changed. I hope this war is over soon and I will be free to return home. It was very thoughtful of you to mention that I was missed at home, but as to my returning before the scrap is over, never, and I am sure you would not think well of me if I dropped out at this stage of the game. What I have seen has made me give up all hopes of this war ending in one or even two years, and it has enabled me to realize that before long, America will need every able-bodied man to protect her from this terrible menace which is ravaging Europe under the nom de plume of "Kultur." Well, as Milton says, "away melancholy, let us have mirth and jollity." So say I. Please remember me to your family when you write, and also to any of my friends with whom you come in contact. It pleases me to remember that it will be Thanksgiving when you receive this letter, so the most appropriate way of leaving you now seems to be to wish you, your family and friends the heartiest and fullest Thanksgiving greetings possible.

Jouy-en-Argonne – November 2nd

Dear Spencer,

I was so glad to hear that you were well and going to a real school. It was so good of you to write to me, and I am glad to say that I noticed your writing and spelling have improved wonderfully. I expect you will be able to spell better than your big brother, who never could spell worth a darn anyway. Ask Mother if you don't believe me. Say, sometime I wish that you would send me one of those pictures that Mr. Reidpath took of you in your overalls. I should like to see you when you were a little boy, because I probably wouldn't recognize you now that you are grown up.

You know I haven't seen a little fellow in a longtime. Everybody who is not a soldier has been taken from their homes a long time ago. All you see is soldiers. All the people who used to live in this district where the fighting is going on had to leave their homes, taking only the things they could carry in their little carts, because the terrible Germans send their awful shells over and destroy everything—homes, people—everything. Nothing is left, not even trees or grass.

Winter is coming on now and the weather is getting bad. It rains almost every day, and there is lots and lots of mud everywhere you look. I am thankful that you and Milton are young so that you will not have to see this life over here.

I am sending you some little pictures which I got out of some cigarettes that I have been compelled to smoke because I have no American tobacco. The pictures are of English soldiers and they are very true to life. I hope you will write to me again soon and tell me about Ruthy and your school work. I also will write to you again shortly.

Jouy-en-Argonne – November 5th

Dear Doctor,

I assure you that my failure to write to you has not been a matter of forgetfulness on my part. I have said to myself many a time, "the doctor will be the one man who will be interested in hearing from me and I must write." But somehow or other, this kind of life does not foster the concentration which is necessary for such a mental effort. Our work is of such a nature that it produces a great mental strain, leaving us when we are relieved from duty mentally and physically fatigued, with very little inclination to carry on the amount of correspondence we all desire. Nevertheless, as is always the case, we look forward to the incoming mail with the greatest of expectancy, and are never so happy as when we receive news of our friends or family.

I rather think that you must have heard indirectly about my work from Father, but probably you would like to hear more of the particulars. Our ambulances are the standard Ford chassis, equipped with a cleverly designed wooden body capable of carrying five sitting cases or three stretcher cases. In every respect these little cars have proven themselves the most practical for the work an ambulance is called upon to do. They are light, fast, powerful on hills, easy to turn around, easily repaired, and they sometimes seem uncanny in their ability to pull you out of tight places. I'll never forget one time my little old Ford came through with glory. I was scooting along a devil of a road one black night with a load of five *blesses*, when my right rear wheel slid down into a shell hole. I gave her all the juice she had, but she could not get a footing. Feeling discouraged I got out of the car, rather alarmed and excited because the number of shells dropping around made it an unhealthy spot to be stationed at.

I pulled the *blessés* out of the back of the car. Then, by reversing and going forward a number of times, as only a Ford can do, the little old bus at last climbed out of the hole. I packed my *blessés* in again and beat a hasty retreat to a more sheltered spot, where I waited until the bombardment had let up a bit. If I had been driving a larger car, I would have been compelled to sit in my ambulance until a truck came along that could pull me out. This would have been rather fatal, for the next morning in passing this same spot, I found it to be within 50 feet of an ammunition depot which the Boche had discovered and destroyed during the night.

Stretcher Bearers at Post 239, with Shorty Mills in the background to the right.

The division to which we are attached is now holding a very important sector in the Verdun front. We have been up here now for four weeks, and it is very probable that we will remain here until the first of January. There is a rumor current that our division will form a unit of the French troops who are to leave for the Italian front in the near future. We all hope that we will be able to stick with our division, so don't be surprised if you hear from me down in the land where every time you turn around you see a day go by. That was a deep one.

Our work right now is comparatively easy. Winter is approaching rapidly, necessitating the partial cessation of hostilities until the spring. When the spring comes we are all looking forward to that great American drive we have been hearing so much about. I will give Pershing credit; he certainly is pushing things ahead with great rapidity. I hear indirectly that American troops have already taken over a small sector, of course heavily supported by French troops, and that we have also put some artillery into action. They are using the French 75 guns, but I am sorry to say that there are a lot of us over here who, having seen as much as we have, are little inclined to think they will have any better success than the French and the English. The longer I stay over here, the greater respect I have for

German thoroughness and efficiency. I am firmly convinced that the German line is impenetrable, and that this war will continue for an indefinite period, or until both sides become so fatigued that they will be glad to both call it quits.

I had the opportunity the other day to visit some ground that the French captured in their last offensive. It was one mess of trenches, and I was surprised to find how superior they were to the French trenches. In addition to these they have numerous tunnels, some 20 to 30 feet underground, well-drained and ventilated and equipped with electric lights. When you consider that they have any number of such positions to fall back upon, you will see why some of us are so pessimistic. In addition to this the Boche are supreme in the air, and I don't think that we will ever be able to perfect a motor which will compare with the German aviation motor. The only thing we can do is to do our bit—either at the front or at home—and hope and pray that something will happen, either a revolution in Germany, or something of that nature that will destroy their morale and bring a close to this endless struggle.

Sous-Officier of 3rd Zouaves.

Jouy-en-Argonne – November 10th

My dear Mother,

I am out at the Montzeville Post tonight as I am writing this letter to you. It has been a very quiet day, only one call so far and that for a sick case. We have just finished our evening meal, if you may call it such. We are issued a small piece of meat and some cabbage each day. In the morning we put our ration together and start them boiling. At noon, we drain off the liquid and have soup with our bread and coffee. In the evening, we have the meat and cabbage with our bread and coffee. This is repeated every day, with the exception that some days we are given potatoes instead of cabbage.

I don't know that I have ever told you about our famous "Hell's Corner." This is a fork in the road, just outside of the town of Montzeville, that has become famous wherever ambulance drivers congregate. All the traffic that is necessary to supply both fronts before Esne and Le Mort Homme must pass this particular fork; the Esne traffic bearing off to

Post at Montzeville.

the left, and the other traffic to the right. It seems that the Boche have an extremely accurate range on this spot and knowing how important it is, shell the fork almost incessantly, hoping to hit some of the traffic that they know has to pass. The result is that they are many times successful, and because of the great number of casualties that have taken place, the fork has acquired its name. But we have learned that the methodical Boche shoots in volleys of five shots. We therefore wait until five shots come over, and then tear past the place.

We have another interesting post, the one at Chattancourt. That poor little town has been reduced to a rubbish heap as a result of constant bombardment over the period of three years. The highest portion of the wreckage left standing is a corner of the building that once housed the office of the telegraph company. Our post is just out of the town, in the ruins of what was once the railroad station of the main line that ran from Verdun to Aachen. The station, of course, is a mass of wreckage, but we have fashioned a very comfortable *abri* on the sight by digging down under the rubbish, and then piling sand bags on top for additional protection.

Well, I will have to leave you now, as one of the cars has just gone by with a load. He came from Post 232, so I will have to run up there and wait for my load of mutilated human flesh. Funny that our very existence as a service depends upon the efficiency of men to tear themselves apart or otherwise maim each other. What is it all about?

Telegraph station at Chattancourt, November 1917.

Famous Hell's Corner, Montzeville.

Jouy-en-Argonne — November 12th

Dear Mr. Rogers,

I received with the greatest of pleasure your kind letter of October 12th. It arrived in this morning's mail; a very pleasant surprise indeed. I really appreciate it a lot more than ordinary letters because of your being a business man, as well as a friend whose time I know to be valuable. Your pleasing description of the activities along the Lake Shore makes me wish more than ever that I was back there once again, enjoying the happy, carefree life that has been mine for so many seasons in the past.

Marion has been very thoughtful in writing to me from time to time. Her last letter was from Wellesley, informing me that she was at last installed in college, and that she enjoyed the work very much. Wasn't it fortunate that she could have two of her best friends, Elsa and Florence, so near her? I was very interested to learn of Mr. Leache's propaganda against the liquor interests in Derby. I hope that I will soon learn that his efforts have been successful. This war is a very, very serious affair, more serious, I'm afraid, than the majority of the people in the States realize, and everything that would in any way hinder the government's preparation should be immediately eliminated. I have had frequent opportunities of late to read American newspapers. Now I tell you, it does me good to learn of what drastic measures the government is taking to fight Pro-Germanism. This is a serious menace which must be gotten rid of before things can be expected to run smoothly.

From what I am able to judge from the newspapers, the feeling of the American people at present is that we are in this war purely with the idea of establishing, for all times, the supremacy of democracy. They have not as yet been forced into that intense hatred, not only against Prussianism but everything pertaining to the German race, that the French and English nations have been compelled to assume. But I ask, what will be the attitude of the people when the lists of our dead and wounded boys reach home, and will they hold this same feeling after two or more years of continuous fighting? I myself have seen sufficient evidence in the past few months to entirely change my feeling of placid disbelief in the reports of atrocities, to one of intense loathing of the very name of "Boche." But on the other hand, the longer one stays over here, the greater respect one gets for German artillery and military tactics. It is because I have seen the effectiveness of their tactics and the wonderful construction of their entrenchments that I, like the majority of the people over here, have little faith in seeing this conflict come to a finish before at least two years. Not a very pleasant outlook, I admit, but a grim reality just the same.

Our work at present is quiet, but I fear it is like a lull before a storm. There are frequent *coups de main* on both sides, alternated with *petit* gas attacks. A *coup de main* is a French expression or term used to describe a trench raid for the purpose of reconnoitering and taking a few prisoners from whom information may be secured. They are usually quite prevalent just before a major offensive, as both sides endeavor in this way to learn as much as possible about the disposition of troops and artillery. It must be admitted that the means of forcing this information from the prisoners are some of the worst aspects of police third degree methods.

Tonight, as I was sitting writing to you, a telephone message came in which necessarily interrupted this letter. Here is the message translated:

"Extremely urgent. Extreme emergency. Headquarters of number -------- The commandant of the cantonment at Montzeville."

"Attack by gas in the zones between hills number 304 and 239 at 2:00 exactly."

You can imagine the excitement this short message stirred up in our little abri. The lieutenant sent a man to carry the message to the occupants of the other *abris* along the road. I went up to my car and got out my gas mask. When I came down again they were all trying on their masks, seeing that they fitted snuggly to their heads. What a grotesque sight they presented. When we satisfied ourselves as to the adaptability of the masks, we sat down with

Kielty at Post 239.

them hanging over our necks and waited. Presently we heard a noise on the stairs. The curtains parted and three men stumbled in, groping blindly in the light of the little room. Yes, the gas was at the upper end of the valley and was gradually creeping our way. The men had been caught without masks and were in bad shape. The doctor, after examining them, said that they would have to be taken to the hospital immediately. With faint heart, I admit, I bundled up, put on my mask, and ascended the stairs. The gassed men came up immediately afterward. I cranked up my old Ford, saw that the men were safely put in the ambulance, and then started for the hospital some nine miles behind the lines.

As I started down the road five gas shells landed nearby. You can tell a gas shell from a high explosive shell by the different noise they make as they explode. Gas shells go off with a soft "flump" and then a sharp "crack," while the high explosives go off with a terrific roar. After running for about half an hour, I noticed that the men I passed on the road had taken off their masks, so I decided to follow suit. It was a great relief to take the mask off, as one's breath clouds up the lenses, making night driving all the more difficult. That night I made six such trips, carrying in all 21 gas cases.

Well, I will have to leave you now as I have to wash my car, a job that must be finished before inspection at dinner. I take this opportunity in closing to wish you and your family the happiest of Christmas greetings.

Loading the car. Flynn and McGrath are in the background.

Jouy-en-Argonne — November 19th

Dear Mother,

I am glad to inform you that I am now receiving your letters quite regularly. The last one that arrived said that you had received my paper knife. I am glad that it arrived safely, because I had some doubts as to whether it would get through the mail. It was nothing much, taking only a few minutes to make, but it was about the only suitable thing I could think of that would get through the mail.

I am sorry that I will be unable to send any Christmas presents home. We have been working out here now for almost two months, so I have not had any opportunity to buy or make anything suitable to send home, and anyway, I would have had to send them off some days ago if they were to arrive at Christmas time. I hope if you have gotten me anything, it has been sent by now and the package is not too large. Numerous packages, small in size, would be more sure to reach me than one large package. I have not received any packages from the States as yet, but hope to receive them soon. Some of the boys have arranged with their families to have a small box of cigarettes, and perhaps some chocolate, sent every week; this system seems the best. Take the three dollars and immediately send me some cigarettes.

The news of home was very interesting. I hope Mr. Leach wins his fight against booze, although I admit that his activities could not be very popular over here. All we get to drink is a poor grade of French wine called *pinard*. We do not dare drink the water as it is all contaminated. I did not know that Will Morgan had taken over the Curtis plant. You've got to hand him credit for the way he has built himself up from nothing.

We have not been doing much work lately, as things have been very quiet on our side of the Meuse River. The majority of the fighting this last month has been to our immediate right, on the right bank of the Meuse, and to our left, a good distance off. The number of *blessés* have been small, however. Indeed, I am quite sure that we carried more *blessés* in the one week at Recicourt during the August attack than we have carried in the whole two months that I've been here. I mean by that, actual wounded, not sick and gas cases. Sometimes the French or the Germans make a *coup de main*, and then there are usually a few casualties. Or again the Germans may decide to send over a few gas shells. When this happens we always get numerous cases, because the French troops often purposely leave off their masks if the gas is the right kind, so that they can be taken back to the hospital. If they stay at the hospital for two days, they are entitled to a permission of one month back in the interior. This seems all wrong, but you somehow can't blame them for getting fed up with it all, and asking for a fairly safe means of escape from the cruel monotony for at least a brief time. One would have all the more understanding if you realize that some of those men have been in this war since the very first days of the battle of the Marne. Some of the men have been over the top as many as 200 times.

Outside of these activities and an occasional barrage, everything is quiet in the daytime especially. However, in the evening there is always a more or less systematic shelling of the roads, especially the crossroads. Not having to do much work, we spend a lot of time just loafing around, reading papers, writing letters and sitting around the fire place just "crabbing." That is the great occupation in the army. First we start in on our own officers and in a little while we end up by telling how we would run this war if we were Pershing. Then somebody will start a gloom session by reading a letter from home, about some dance or dinner party. This usually breaks up the party and we either go to bed or up on the hill and fool around with our cars.

The other night, when our squad was on reserve, we got a call to go to another sector and help that section in evacuating the wounded. We worked from 2:00 that night until 5:00 the next afternoon, carrying about 90 *blessés* in about seven trips. The Boche had made an attack early in the evening and had gained some ground. But the French had regained it almost immediately by a successful counterattack that had been executed before the Germans had been able to put over a counter-barrage. Little incidents like this and frequent gas attacks come as a welcome break in the monotony of our work.

The taking over of our service by the government has changed things slightly but not to our advantage. We are having trouble about getting our rations, but this will be remedied as soon as Battershell returns from Paris where he has been to procure his commission in the regular army. We were quite excited the other day to hear that there is a possibility of our going down to Italy with our division. This has been denied because America has not declared war on Austria and no American troops are allowed to partake in the Italian campaign. But our French lieutenant received advice that, as the United States would undoubtedly declare war in the near future, we were to be prepared to leave at a minute's notice. Both the French and the English are sending troops to the Italian border to help stem the German advance. Everyone over here is very much disappointed over this unexpected reversal of the Italians. It is the opinion of many that this defeat will put the end of the war back a year. The only bright prospect I have to report is that finally Pershing is pushing forward his preparation for the spring campaign. American engineers have operated the railroads back of the sector now for about two months. They are doing good work. It is also reported that our boys have taken over a small sector and have already suffered some casualties. They caught one German prisoner, but for some reason the poor chap died at the hospital. This will have to be enough for tonight as I am rather tired and have to go on duty tomorrow. If I do not get a chance to write again soon, I will wish you all the best of Christmas greetings. I hate to think of being away from you all at Christmas but as we say over here *"C'est la guerre."* It can't be helped.

Montzeville — November 20th

Dear Red,

I received your letter today just before going out on duty, so I am writing now from the post. I have just finished dinner, and it was as good a one as we ever get. Mashed potatoes, tough beef steak, a hunk of bread, some cheese that was a bit ripe, a cup of *pinard* and a cup of tea with a shot of rum to warm us up a bit. The Frenchmen have cleaned up the table and are now playing cards for big stakes. They sometimes lose as much as three cents in one hand, and the other night one of them won two Francs (40 cents). They wanted me to play, but I was afraid the excitement would give me a weak heart, so I declined in my best grade of French. One night they "roped" me into the game, and beat me out of eighteen cents, so I am off the game for good.

Gee! You are a rotten writer. It took me about half an hour to figure out your letter. But don't think I don't appreciate your letters just the same. I've got to depend on you for a lot of news I can't get from anyone else, so please write more regularly even if I am sometimes unable to reply immediately. Yes, I must admit I know a Ford now. Our mechanic is a lazy son of a gun, so he had our lieutenant send out the order that we have to do all the repairs on our cars ourselves. I have taken the whole "darn" thing apart and put it together again. Our old busses get terribly hard usage because the roads are so bad, we carry such heavy loads and there are so many hills, so I have to look after the cars a lot more than I did in the States. We have to spend the whole day after we come in from duty in washing, oiling and greasing, and fixing up the old bus.

Say, from what you tell me, I should judge that there was something the matter with the ignition system on your old Ford. Probably, your magneto contact point is dirty. Take out the contact pole in the top of your magneto case. If that does not remedy the matter, go over your electric system and see if you have any loose connections or a short circuit. If nothing happens then, test your spark plugs with a hammer. Probably the plugs are dirty or the porcelains are broken. If you do all these things, you ought to find the trouble. It might be a good idea to clean your commutator. I wouldn't oil it more than once a week. Don't be afraid to fuss with the old bus, it's the only way that you can learn anything about it. Keep your springs well oiled. I broke a rear spring the other day, and I caught hell from the lieutenant because it wasn't oiled enough.

This letter was necessarily interrupted here because the other car just came down from the Chattencourt Post with a load of wounded, and I had to take his place. It is not a very dark night, although neither the moon nor the stars are out, but I was able to see sufficiently well to avoid most of the shell holes and to see the passing ammunition trains.

It's pretty quiet tonight, too. There is only one battery going, at our left. It fires six shots about every three minutes. A couple of Boche shells landed but were far enough from the road not to throw any dirt or *éclat* on my car. As long as they keep that far away I don't give a damn, but when they land in the road in front of you, then I have the fear of God in my heart. I think that you can understand what I mean.

I'll never forget one time when two of us were going out to relieve the post. Mills was about two hundred yards in front of me and we were going like hell around a bend in the road, which was in sight of the bastard Germans. All of a sudden I see a cloud of smoke and dirt in the woods ahead where Mills' car had been a moment ago, and Mills' car seemed to have completely disappeared. Well, you can guess how I felt. I was sure that the shell had hit Mills' car and had blown him to the happy hunting grounds. I ran along slowly very much unnerved, expecting to have to pick old Mills up with a spoon, but when I had pretty nearly reached the scene of the supposed disaster, the smoke cleared away, and to my relief, I saw Mills' car beating it around the hill, hell bent for election. Then I saw what had happened. The shell had hit in the road just behind his car, and of course I could not see him on account of the smoke.

I must tell you about our posts. The first one is at a little village (Montzeville), nestled behind a hill, out of sight of the Boche. The next (Esne) is what is left of another village on the other side of the hill. In order to get to the second post we have to travel a road that goes around the hill. As the first line of trenches are in the valley and the Boche hold the opposite hill, this road is in direct sight of the Germans, who are about a quarter of a mile away. We call this bend around the hill "Hell's Corner." Day traffic over this road is absolutely forbidden but when there are any *grave blessés* we have to travel it just the same.

Well, I have got to leave you now because four gassed men just came in, and I have to take them to the hospital right away. I wish you and the family the best of Christmas greetings, and I sure hope that you will be thinking of me on Christmas day. You know how much I will be thinking of you. Hit your lessons a good hard one and be careful of yourself. If you ever have any spare money you might send me some Bull or some P.A. See if you can get Mrs. Snyder to send me some tobacco or cigarettes. Well, give my best to everyone and write once in a while.

PS. I received a letter from Hamilton (French teacher) the other day. He is in YMCA work.

Village of Esne, Verdun, 1917.

In the hills of France – November 21st

Dear Miss McIntosh,

I am really at a loss to express my appreciation of your letter of the twenty-seventh of October which arrived yesterday. One does not realize how numerous and how thoughtful are his friends until he is separated from them for any length of time. I enjoyed your letter all the more because it was so full of interesting news that I was heretofore ignorant of. It must have been a very inspiring sight indeed to see our boys of the 74th Regiment in their farewell march. I am afraid that it would not have been such a joyous occasion if the boys knew what they were to encounter over here.

It does me good to hear how splendidly Buffalo is responding to the Second Liberty Loan. The news of such ready support of the government produces a great moral effect on the French people, making their tremendous burden rest lighter on their shoulders.

I must take this opportunity to set you aright about that hospital incident you referred to. It is true that the Germans bombed and destroyed the hospital at Vadelaincourt. In fact, we visit this hospital almost every day in our work. But as to your story about the doctor who sent to the German line and told the Boche where to get off, well, that is so absurd that it provokes me to laughter. The mere lifting of one's helmet ever so little above the earthworks would be sufficient to bring a shower of German death-laden bullets at that very spot, let alone boldly exposing one's whole person to those ever watchful, fiendish eyes of the Boche sharpshooters.

It might interest you to learn the true story about the bombing of the hospital at Vadelaincourt, which is a small town on the railroad, near Verdun. Several days before the Germans made their raid on the hospital, which by the way the French had unwisely located near an ammunition depot in the outskirts of the town, they sent aeroplanes over the lines which dropped printed notices on the hospital grounds saying that if the French authorities had not moved the hospital at the end of six days that it could be destroyed by bombs. The French, nothing daunted, immediately sent word to the Germans by similar channels that they had a battery of their cannons trained on a large German base hospital, and if the French hospital was molested in any way they would straightaway destroy the German hospital with their guns. Six days passed and the seventh was also tranquil, so the French authorities began to feel that nothing further would happen, but on the evening of the eighth day the Boche planes bombed the hospital for three solid hours, killing a number of nurses, doctors and patients and reducing the hospital to ruins. Now whether or not the French lived up to their threat, I never heard, but I think it was a bluff on their part that the Germans had known enough to call. This is a good example of modern warfare.

I will not bother to tell you of our work in detail, as you have probably read the letters I have sent home. Things are, as you said, rather quiet now, but this does not mean that the Germans are weakening. On the contrary, they look as undefeatable as ever to me. The main reason for the suspension of hostilities is that Jack Frost is gradually gripping the land in his icy, cold fingers, making it impossible for either side to conduct a successful campaign, until the spring makes Old Man Winter loosen his grip. By then we will see Uncle Sam in action.

We are fairly well quartered and fed, but as the holiday season draws near we all are feeling prey to a more or less serious attack of homesickness, but we are comforted to some extent by the frequent letters from home and the knowledge that we are missed as much as we miss being with you. We all try to forget our discomforts and endeavor to remember for what a great cause and for what a wonderful country we are giving our services, and the gist of our hopes and prayers is that the terrible conflict will come to a speedy and just end, leaving us free once more to join our family and friends in that same quiet state which prevailed before this world was driven into such a strife, all to please the unnatural ambition of one, selfish, greedy man.

I will take the opportunity in closing to wish you, your family and friends the best of Christmas greetings, and it is of course needless to add that I hope to hear from you soon.

A 220mm trench mortar on a transporter at Érize, 1917.

Part 3

Winter of 1917–1918

Introduction

Despite heavy losses of merchant vessels bringing vital supplies to Britain, the lifelines of trade, particularly to the United States, remained open. At the same time the Allied blockade of German ports in the Baltic and North Seas was having a measurable effect on the German war effort.

America produced most of the ordnance for the Allied war effort.[6] The U.S. manufactured 2,000,000 artillery rounds for use in the war, as well as 10,000 tons of poisonous gas, and 600,000 Springfield rifles had been shipped overseas before the design and manufacturing process of the British Enfield rifle was completed.[7] American industry also manufactured 3.5 billion rounds of small arms ammunition, of which 1.8 billion were shipped to Europe.

For Royce Wolfe, the winter months were a time of seemingly endless physical hardship and cold boredom, relieved by occasional calls to transport the wounded. His letters of early winter, with the approach of the Christmas holidays, reveal a heightened sense of homesickness along with an unwavering resolve to see the matter through.

[6]. Ayers, The War with Germany, 83

[7]. Ayers, The War with Germany, 72

Jouy-en-Argonne – December 1st

My Dear Mother,

I received your letter of November 6th just a few days ago, and I say as usual, I cannot understand why you do not receive my letters more regularly. Thanksgiving of 1917 has passed, being the second festival of the harvest that I have spent away from you. Although we all felt the absence from our friends and families more or less deeply, we did the best, considering our opportunities, to make the day as homelike as possible. In the first place, the government promised us a turkey. Well we waited expectantly for that bird to come until the twenty-eighth, when we all became worried over its non-arrival, so our officers set out on a search for a substitute, and what a time they had. It was their intention to secure a goose, but after several vain attempts at the few farmhouses in the interior that kept these species of birds, they decided that chicken would have to be the substitute.

The search for the chicken, one that would be suitable to eat, was equally as hard but the search had better results. One old lady replied that as her roosters were married to her chickens, she could not dispose of them. Another said that if she sold her chickens she would not be able to get any more. But finally they were able to get hold of five for which they paid something like two dollars and a half apiece.

The French cook was given a holiday and one of our boys, Loony Pond, was crowned cook for the day. The three of us stayed up all night making the proper preparations. The task of preparing the chickens fell to me. I killed, picked, cleaned and quartered the chickens after the

Gordon Rogers with chickens for Thanksgiving, 1917.

manner that I learned from watching you, so you see that even if I was in your way when you used to prepare the Thanksgiving dinner, I nevertheless absorbed enough knowledge to make myself useful over here. I remember how I used to shudder as you pulled out the birds' insides when I was doing the same this time without winking an eye.

After working all that night and the next morning, we served dinner only a half an hour late. Here is the menu: Oyster boullion, fried chicken, mashed potatoes. dumplings, real thick gravy, creamed onions, lobster salad, lemon pie, Swiss cheese, nuts, coffee and champagne. Some dinner, and we had that bunch of thirty-six fellows so full when we finished that they hardly could get up. It was a lot of work and it cost a lot of money, spoiling the best part of $75.00, but it certainly was worthwhile. Pond was a great success, and not a thing turned out bad. The only trouble we had was that we had such an insufficient supply of dishes to serve everything. I myself was so full that I had to go to bed after dinner and stay there all day. The French *medicine chef* of our division ate dinner with our officers. They say that he can't get over the wonderful feast he had.

Things have been more active on the front this last week. Four of our cars have been doing extra work in another sector, and today our section has taken over three new posts. One is at what is left of the little village of Chattancourt, another is at the village of Esne, and another is an artillery post to the right of Montzeville. So we will be at our posts now every two days for 24 hours. We have hopes that our division will soon go *en repos* because it is getting very cold and disagreeable to drive. Having no wind-shield, the snow and sleet hits our faces and makes it almost impossible to keep our eyes open. This physical discomfort, added to the fact that all our driving at night is without lights, makes our trips,

Winter of 1917–18.

both night and day, very uncomfortable.

I certainly shall enjoy a good hot bath once we get back of the lines. There is absolutely no water to even drink, let alone wash in. It is so cold that I haven't had my clothes off now for over six weeks. My underwear fairly sticks to me. And I must admit that, along with every other member of the section and all the Frenchmen, I am lousy as hell. In fact, I am so ridiculous that I am unable to get to sleep at night until I have made a vain attempt to kill as many as possible of the little so-and-sos.

While I was at post the other night at 252, I felt rather foolish, so I decided that I should be a "poet." Here is the result, a pathetic little ditty entitled,

"A Night at the Post":
The night was drear, the sky was clear,
The roar of guns was deafening;
While to our right the blaze of lights
Announced the fight impending.

A star-like light that paused in flight
A moment ere departing.
Illumined night's grey, ghastly gloom;
A spectacle tres startling.

Below we sat like rats in trap
Enjoying "l'abri's" shelter.
A'reading full how English bull
Drove murdering Boche a'skelter.

The night grew on and memories fond
Of days "avant la guerre"
Made minds fatigued, recall with ease
Sweet face and wavy hair.

But such sweet dreams it always seems
Are bound to be disrupted.

A step is heard upon the stairs;
My thoughts are interrupted.

"Qui est-ce" the doctor sharply cries,
As from his snooze he stirs.
We all do start as curtains part;
Brancardier Lure appears.

With faltering pace he gropes in space,
The light it does near blind him.
A moment more, then he reports,
"Trois blessés grave: mon Capitan."

The doctor in his cordial way
Welcomes the old "brancardier."
"*Une voiture* prompt," his orders say
To us who stand there gaping.

With hearts astir, we climb the stairs,
To where our Ford is rested.
A couple turns, the '*essence*' burns,
The motor seems well tested.

With careful hands the sturdy band
Lift stretchers three in place.
The back is shut, we get speed up
And slowly fade in space.

So it is always with us here
Who do our bit of service.
'Tis love of country, home and friends,
That gives us zest for service.

Foolish, isn't it, but it isn't as bad as some that I have attempted before. I am all out of paper, so please excuse the odds and ends.

I suppose that this should be my Christmas letter to you even if it is only December the First. Thanksgiving was bad enough, but I hate to think of spending Christmas away from you all, and I must remember that I am only one of many thousands who will suffer and suffer bravely this enforced separation. I assure you that my thoughts will be with you that day, and I hope that my absence will not take away from your happiness. Just remember that this is a time of dire necessity, when our country and homes are menaced as never before, and, when you do think of me, let it not be with remorse, but with that proud, happy feeling that comes to every American mother who has lent her boy to the greatest of all causes, the cause of our great country.

It will not be long, I hope, before the nations of the earth succeed in destroying this hideous power which threatens humanity and if I am permitted to come home at that time, I will appreciate you all the more, so I hope you will have reason to be justly proud of me.

So brace up, little Mother. Do not think of the dark side but of the bright, and that side will come soon, I am sure. Be cheery and hopeful, as every good American mother should be, and when Christmas day does come, let home be filled with joy and happiness as never before.

PS. I received a wonderful package from Marion Rogers the other day for which I have written and thanked her. I have not received your package as yet, but I hope that it was not lost. Wish that you could hear the rats in the *abri* as I write this to you. There must be hundreds of them. They run up and down the tin roof like a herd of sheep. You must cover your face with a blanket when you lay down to sleep or else they will run over your face. They are so ravenous that they will eat right through your pockets in order to get to some piece of food that might be lying there. What between the rats and lice, we have a great life.

Battery of 220mm at fire.

Jouy-en-Argonne, December — 9th

My Dear Mother,

I received your letter of November sixth a few days ago, but I have been so busy lately that I have been unable to write. In addition to taking over two new posts, we are having to continue with our regular triage work and have resumed service at one of our old posts. We have also been extremely unfortunate in losing four of our boys who are now in the hospital. No, nothing serious. Two of the fellows are hideous sights, boils from head to foot. Their blood has undoubtedly been poisoned by eating bad tinned food. Gordon Rogers broke a rib or two when he fell into some ruins. The hardest bit of luck concerns the loss of our mechanic at a time when nearly all the cars are rolling continuously and three of them are *en panne*. Flynn tore a muscle in his leg while bringing in a broken down car. They are all resting very comfortably in the American hospital at Fleury, and thankful that they didn't have to go to one of the French hospitals. Some of us see them every day and they return with wonderful stories about the marvelous food that the boys are receiving at the hospital.

The hospital is connected with a camp of American Army engineers who partly operate the railroads in this sector. It has got to be quite a usual sight to see American uniforms and their new helmets in these parts. Like all Americans, the boys are terribly inquisitive and they are continuously skipping away from their camps to come up here at the front, in quest of excitement. This afternoon, I was sitting in our *abri* at Montzeville, enjoying a smoke after a very good meal, when I was startled almost to death by a hollering at the entrance of the *abri*, "Can anybody here speak English?" Well, you can rest assured that I lost no time in answering in the affirmative, and immediately climbed to the surface to find three Americans at the entrance. They looked very funny in their misfit uniforms and funny-shaped steel helmets. The helmets look a lot like the English helmet but are flatter and broader and are set high on the head. The American government had run short of service coats so they have been compelled to issue Canadian tunics to their soldiers. We received an issue of them the other day and I must say that they are a lot better looking then the regular American tunic, and they are also a lot more comfortable. After hearty greetings, they explained that they had beat it away from their camp and were intent on seeing what there was to see of the trenches. I persuaded them to enter the *abri* for a moment or two, and then I explained to them that as it was a very bright day, the journey would be rather difficult as well a dangerous, so we would be compelled to stick to the communication trenches and could not attempt to make short cuts across the land. But this attempt to discourage them finally proved useless, and as they very gently put it up to me, I agreed to show them something worthwhile.

So I took them up to see the tunnels of Mort Homme. It is quite a walk and most of it is in sight of the German lines, but the boys were game all the way through. As it was their first experience of shell and machine gun fire, I had a great time in observing their faces when they would fling themselves down in the mud when a shell landed close by or when one would whistle by uncomfortably close. One of the fellows, who by the way, was a long lanky westerner who had punched cows before coming over here, presented the funniest sight in the world when he crawled along on his hands and knees, at the places in the communicating trenches where the parapets were too low to walk upright in. They were all astonished at the thorough way the Germans had built the tunnels. We walked through the whole length of the largest one, and I showed them the lighting and ventilating plant, the hospital and all the wonderful little rooms the German officers had fixed up along the sides of the tunnel. It is a wonderful piece of engineering and I wish that I could describe how

75mm anti-aircraft gun.

thoroughly the Germans have built it. If you get a chance to read a newspaper or magazine description of it, please do, and remember that I have seen it all and even have as a souvenir the name of the tunnel, printed in large type, that an officer gave me permission to take from the entrance of the tunnel.

The trip back was easier as it was then fairly dark. One of the fellows picked up a German skull from one of the skeletons lying about the hill. It had a large hole in it, right over the temple where a piece of *éclat* had probably entered. We arrived back at Montzeville at about dinner time, 4:50, and after resting a few moments, the boys started for their camp at Fleury, thanking me for the little favor.

After dinner, Doc Loomis came through with a load, so I had to go up to 232 where I am writing this letter. Doc arrived back a little while ago, but as he was tired, he has gone to sleep. The night driving strains your eyes. I was driving along the other night, very slowly of course, when I thought I saw something in the road immediately in front of me. I slammed on my brakes and to my surprise, I found that I hadn't been moving at all. My foot had unconsciously pushed the lever into neutral and my eyes were in such a condition that they were unable to recognize the fact that I was standing still. This has happened lots of times, especially when I am physically tired. You seem to lose all sense of movement. Also, sometimes you will be driving along and all of a sudden everything will get black in front of you. You will have to stop the car until the spell passes. I had one of those spells the other night and before I could regain my sight, a *camion* busted into me and nearly shoved me over the bank. So my car doesn't look as nice as the one in the picture I sent to you.

It looks now as if we will go *en repos* in about fifteen days. We are about due for a rest as we have been up here now for about three months. As we haven't enough men in the section, our lieutenant has been unable to let us take our regular permissions. These, I hope, will come when our division is *en repos*. It is rumored that after an indefinite *repose*, our division will go to Italy and it seems likely that we will go with them. I hear it is warm down there, and we will all welcome a change from this wet, cold weather we are having here. Well, anyway, I hope we get some rest soon as we are all getting rather tired out. Working every other twenty-four hours is no cinch, believe me.

Say, I would like to have *beaucoup* pairs of heavy socks, the heavier the better, and send them as soon as possible. I received an express order for some money the other day and I don't know where it came from. If it is the gift of Uncle Charlie which you mentioned in your letter, I want you to thank him for me from the bottom of my heart. There are so many little things like jelly, butter, cookies, etc. that a fellow has to have to be comfortable and which cost like the very devil. I really don't know how to thank Charlie, but please try to convey to him my deepest feelings of gratitude and appreciation.

It seems that you have at last got the right dope on 21 rue Raynouard. They are the rottenest bunch of thieves and rascals the Lord ever made, and our famous chief, A.P. Andrews, is the biggest crook of them all. I have never received a package from you yet, and I lay it all to that bunch. Some day the whole organization is going to be exposed and then there will be some smell raised. From all I hear the Red Cross isn't nearly as bad, but I guess there is a certain amount of graft there too. But everything has changed lately as the government has taken all these various services and is exercising strict control over them.

The other night the Germans bombed the headquarters of the Second Army at Souilly. The funny part of it is that the only damage that they did was in a camp that held the German prisoners that were working on the roads in that vicinity. Several Germans were killed and a lot more wounded. This gave us all a big chuckle. I have bought a couple of very nice vases for you. The Frenchmen make them out of *soixante-quinze* shells. They take the empty shell and after filling it with some substance, they hammer it into very beautiful

Bill Wholey and French Lieutenant in tent at Jouy.

designs. The result is quite good looking.

Well, I hope you all passed a most pleasant Christmas and enjoyed your holiday season. I am hoping that we will be relieved so that we can spend Christmas back of the lines, *en repos*. If seven of our boys are compelled to be out at post it will break up our plans for a celebration.

Your letters are never dull, and tell Dad that I wish that he would write more often. Certainly am pleased to hear that Milton has been elected president of his class at Nichols. Tell Spencer that I have lost my pup, but I expect to get another soon.

Jouy-en-Argonne — December 14th

My Dear Aunt Al,

It did seem so good to hear from you. I received your letter of October 30th yesterday, it having taken an extremely long time in reaching me. For some unaccountable reason, all the mail has been delayed lately. It is very annoying to say the least. The mail service is very irregular. I have received notice that many packages have been sent to me, but at this date I have received only one. I do hope they have not all been lost.

News of Eden interests me so much. It did me good to hear how nobly your little village responded to the Second Liberty Loan. When we over here heard how quickly and with what little effort that huge sum of money was raised, it gave us a new strength for our work because it showed beyond a doubt that the American people are behind us heart and soul, and God only knows we need to be heartened because the monotony of this life, and the hardships we endure, tend to make us listless and discontented with our lot. That is why we all crave for news of home and appreciate the occasional packages from our friends and the Red Cross which we receive at long intervals.

Winter has set in with a vigor. Our work continues with a slight change. Two new posts have been added to our routine which increases our work. We now work for twenty-four hours every other day. The new posts are very comfortable, but a trifle more dangerous than the other posts on our beat. Although they are in full view of the Germans, whose trenches are but half a mile away, we have not as yet been troubled by being shot at deliberately, although the roads are continually under fire, so the Boche in this way hopes to destroy the ammunition and supply trains that are almost always passing along the roads. If the Germans did fire at our cars I would not feel that they did not have some justification. French officers will drive up as near the front as they think is safe and then instead of walking the rest of the way, they will commandeer one of our cars and make us take them up to the front. This is a decided breach of etiquette. But there is nothing that we can do about it.

With the exception of a few *coups de main*, which bring forth barrages from both sides almost nightly, the front at this point is rather quiet. The number of *blessés* is pleasingly small, but numerous cases of trench feet have come in. The feet become swollen and very painful from being cold and wet for long periods of time. In many cases this affliction is more painful than a wound. Here is where the Red Cross can do its best work by supplying plenty of warm socks to keep the feet warm and dry.

French observation balloon at Jouy.

We have been working up in this sector now for about three months. Our division will probably be going *en repos* soon and we are all looking forward to that time as we need rest badly.

We hope to be out of here and behind the lines before Christmas so that we'll be together for that day at least. We have disposed of our French cook, and one of our boys has taken the job over, much to our relief, as we will now be able to get some real American cooking. French cooking is too greasy as a steady diet.

Christmas of 1917 will be a thing of the past when you receive this letter, and, although I have written you a Christmas letter, I will wish you the best of Christmas greetings again in case my previous letter does not reach you. I would like to be home with you all for that day, but I know you will all be thinking of me even if I am not there. I enjoy your letters ever so much and hope you will write more often.

Love and best wishes for you and Charlie.

Jouy-en-Argonne – December 16th

My Dear Mother,

I am feeling rather out of spirits tonight. My old tin can has broken down and I have been compelled to telephone into our barracks to have them send out a new set of wires. There is a short circuit somewhere which I have not been able to find. I was fortunate enough to get the old bus into the hospital at Fleury and I am now waiting for the relief to arrive. This is just a note to let you know that I am well and thinking of you, so it will be short. Our work continues to be light, but it is rumored that an attack is to come soon. I hope we

Boche airplane brought down near Souilly.

will be back *en repos* before that time comes because the weather is getting bitterly cold and the driving extremely disagreeable. Had a little excitement this morning when I witnessed the fall of two Boche planes which were successfully attacked by a squad of French planes. The Boche happened to land near the road on which I was traveling. I stopped to see what remained of the wreckage, and was able to get some pieces of the machine as souvenirs. The Boche pilots were a mass of pulp. I wish the French could do something like this all the time.

I am anxiously awaiting my Christmas box. I hope it will arrive before Christmas. Did you receive the cable that I sent you? Please pardon the writing, as I am writing under difficulties due to a sprained wrist which I received from cranking my car. Nothing serious. Two of the boys are in the hospital still. The others are back with the section again. I have taken to wearing *sabots* or wooden shoes. I find them quite the thing in walking around. I wear a heavy pair of sheep-skin slippers which just fit into the wooden shoes. When I am driving or in the quarters I take the wooden shoes off and go around in the slippers. Write soon, love to all and kisses for Spencer.

Jouy-en-Argonne – December 17th

My Dear Friends,

The thought that I have so many friends and that they are all thinking of me heartens me immeasurably, and I must admit I was rather down in the boots when I received your kind letter yesterday. I had just come in from a forty-eight hour run. I was cold, hungry and thoroughly fatigued. While returning from the hospital to our post at the front, my little old Ford went *en panne* due undoubtedly to a short circuit in the magneto. Unfortunately, I found myself practically isolated in a stretch of road very seldom used at night and quite a distance from a telephone station. As we have strict orders never to leave our cars, no matter what the emergency, I settled down to await some passer-by who could take my message to our barracks. This proved a long, cold wait, but presently a Frenchmen came along, and after using my best grade of French, I finally made him understand what I wished of him. On account of some delay in the transmission of the message, relief did not arrive until 5:00 the next day. Considering that there were three inches of snow on the ground, a cold wind blowing and that I had nothing to eat during my wait, I think that you will be able to see why I was rather out of spirits when I returned to our headquarters.

But this, of course, was unusual. We have really nothing to complain about as to our quarters or food. We are cantoned in the empty loft of a barn. The fellows have fixed up two old oil barrels as stoves, and with these we succeed in taking the chill off of the air, although when the wind blows you would be surprised to see how many little crevices spring into existence. Bed is the warmest and most comfortable place we have, and we all retreat to the warmth of our blankets whenever we get a chance. Although it is now only 7:00, we are nearly all in bed. A few of the boys are lingering around one of the fires, slowly disrobing. They present a very amusing sight, and a stranger would be at a loss to understand their peculiar actions; some are sitting, some standing, but all have their undershirts off and are slowly going over them as if they were looking for something. Occasionally the silence is interrupted by, "I've found another," and then the search is suspended while the rest of the fellows crowd around the fortunate hunter and make remarks such as "Gee! he's a big one," "That's your fourteenth, isn't it?" or "I've found only eight tonight." And then the hunt goes on until under examination, the shirts appear to be reasonably free from visitors. Who these little creatures are I leave to your imagination. It is not my intention to relate to you stories of shot and shell on which you must be pretty well fed up. This is a time when everyone should wear a smile, even if one doesn't feel like it. The blacker the situation, the broader the smile. I'm absolutely convinced that the Kaiser will never win this war, because I have never seen a picture of him smiling. It's the man with a smile who always comes through. The best lesson our boys learn over here is to "Grin and bear it." That to me is the great lesson of the war. So, it is the American boys with the smile who will eventually break through the Hindenburg line and enter conquered Germany with a broader smile than ever before.

I thank you all for the kind interest you have taken in me. It is such letters as Mr. Farrar's that make a fellow forget all the discomforts under which he may be suffering and recall to mind the greatness of the people and the principle he may be called upon to sacrifice himself for. So, it is with a braver heart than usual that I bid you *au revoir*, hoping as I do that I may again hear from you all in the near future.

Jouy-en-Argonne – December 20th

My Dear Mother,

Your letter of November 16 and the one of the 29th arrived in yesterday's mail—nice long ones and so full of news. I will try to answer some of your questions.

I received the money that Dad sent. Of course, I was grateful for it, but I wanted it sent from my own money, not Dad's. I still have it as none of us has been allowed to go on permission on account of the shortage of men. We have just enough men to run the cars. I have received three packages, one from Marion, one from Else and the one you sent through Canada. Yours was a fine box and contained sugar, dates, figs, cake and canned goods. It was awfully good of you to send it. Your account of all the many things that have been sent to me certainly pleases yours truly. If I ever receive them, I certainly will be a contented boy. How wonderful it is that everybody is so thoughtful. I will never be able to express my gratitude to them all, and I certainly intend to write to them all if they only think to enclose their addresses.

I have nothing new to tell you. Our work is very light, necessitating only one car on each of the two posts and two cars at triage. Our schedule has changed so that now we only work every four days. The weather continues very cold. We have to execute the greatest of care in driving as the roads are extremely slippery. It is very hard to get the cars going in the morning, but we are very foxy in this respect. We park the cars on a hill, and when we drive off in the morning, we only have to take the stones from under the wheels and off we go. I have collected quite a stack of photos, about three hundred, which I wish I could get to you. They are very interesting. I have also collected numerous souvenirs, such as Boche helmets, skulls, arms, buttons, relics from many ruined places that I have visited… French sabers, guns, and insignia. They make quite a bundle, but I hope I will get them home some day.

Christmas cards and letters have started to arrive, which are all very pretty and make me wish I was back home again. The cook is gathering things for the Christmas dinner. It is going to be some dinner from all reports. The government has promised to send turkey for the occasion. Prospects of going *en repos tout suite* are very slim right now. Everything looks as if we will be here for another month at least. Of course this means we will not be able to go on permission. Our lieutenant has telegraphed for more men to fill out the section, but has received word that the office is short of men at the present time, but that

Kitchen at Jouy-en-Argonne.

they will send out reliefs as soon as they are available. Tough luck.

I am glad to see that Al Prehm is engaged to Catherine Cook. He certainly deserves such luck. It seems to me that everyone I ever knew is either getting married or engaged. I hope that somebody will be left when I get home.

I wish that you wouldn't think that my impromptu leaving for France was a mistake on my part. You know as well as I do that I would never be able to wait until I was old enough to enter the training camps. Moreover, I have no desire to shoulder the responsibilities of a commission even if one was to be obtained. I can serve my country as a private every bit as good as an officer. I am contented with my lot and I beg of you not to think of my step in this respect as a mistake. Just be glad that your son is not a slacker, to my opinion the lowest thing imaginable.

How I wish you would be patient if you don't receive another letter until after an interval, as I am going to attempt to answer all the Christmas correspondence which has already arrived and will probably arrive in the next ten days. It's going to be some task, believe me. Did you think of putting in a pair of fleece-lined foot coverings when you sent my package? They would be awfully warm and comfortable. I could wear them with my wooden shoes. Oh, I didn't tell you I had a pair, did I? It was funny getting used to them, but they are the warmest things on earth. I never thought that I would ever be wearing such things. It was my idea that only the Dutch wore them, but everyone wears them here in the winter.

The offensive next spring promises to be a terrific onslaught. Extensive preparations are already underway: strong *abris* are being built, immense quantities of ammunition are being concentrated at numerous depots near the front, officers are continually passing along the front, studying the ground and looking for promising positions to take or occupy. In the interior, thousands of troops are in training besides the thousands of Americans who are also getting into fighting condition. Without a doubt, this is going to be the deciding campaign of the war. I cannot see how the Germans are going to withstand this onslaught. French, English, Italians and Americans will be united and will act in one body, throwing their tremendous, irresistible forces in one mass against the Germans. How can we be anything but successful? This has got to be the last year of the war. France, as well as England, is in a deplorable state, in comparison to the flourishing countries that they were before the war. The countries can't stand and the people won't stand for another year of war. It has got to come to a finish, so let us pray and hope that we will come out on the top of the heap.

I am pretty sleepy tonight, and, as I go on duty tomorrow, I think that I'll turn into that bunk of mine and call it a day. I still probably need a lot of sleep. I always enjoy the thought of going to bed (quite a difference, I can hear you say, to the Royce of old) because bed is the one warm spot we have. It really wasn't necessary to bring blankets with me as we are able to secure any number of them from the hospitals, gratis, ostensibly for the use of the *blessés*. These blankets are not very clean, but if we are careful not to get them near our faces, they answer the purpose of keeping us warm. We have to be very careful not to get contaminated by the blankets as it is very easy to contract a disease called Le Galle. This is a peculiar little bug that burrows under the skin and is very itchy. The more you itch the more the thing spreads. The only cure is to go to one of the hospitals where they scrape the infected part with a wire brush until the skin is raw, and then they bathe the infected part with a solution of raw sulfur. You can imagine how painful that would be.

The gasoline in my *briquet* is getting rather low, so I think that I will have to stop writing soon. These *briquets* are indispensable as they give us our only light. We make them out of old shell cases and other things. We make smaller ones which we use as cigarette lighters. All the French soldiers do the same, and as the only way for them to get gasoline for their lighters is to get some from us, we are being almost continually asked for *un peu d'essence* as they say. French matches are a government monopoly, and they are therefore very scarce and expensive. Even when you are able to secure some, they do not light many times, and when they do they smell terribly.

Well don't worry about little old me. I have learned how to take care of myself by now. I even wash behind my ears, that is, when I do wash, which is about once a week. Outside of a slight cold in my head, I am feeling very well and seem to be in excellent health. Before this light goes out I will have to go on my nightly hunt for cooties. They seem unusually active tonight and as they have a habit of keeping one awake, I think that I had better leave you now and see what I can find. Give my love to Dad, Milt and Spencer and ask them to write. Also give my best to all my friends who have been so kind to me.

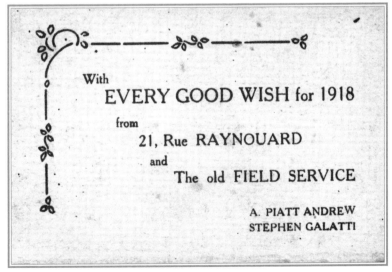

Cards enclosed in billfold. Present from 21 rue Raynouard, Christmas 1917–1918.

Jouy-en-Argonne – December 26th

Christmas of 1917 has passed amid such unusual surroundings that I am at a loss to tell you about it. The day broke cold and clear, and, as I was scheduled to go to post during the afternoon, I was up early, working on my car. I found that the French do not celebrate the day as we do, reserving most of their gift giving and general holiday spirit for New Year's day. The kitchen force was busy all morning long, preparing dinner. And it was a good one. No turkeys arrived, but we had plenty of chicken, fresh vegetables and the usual trimmings that accompany a typical American dinner.

During the morning, a few of the boys motored over to the church at Bethincourt where the French were conducting a service. The church was partially in ruins, the roof over the chancel having been shot off, and several large gaps in the north side of the building gave evidence of the Boche's attempt to demolish the structure. The steeple was still standing, but it had been hit a few times and the clock in the belfry was hanging in some mysterious way to the tower. The main body of the church was full of soldiers in their muddy uniforms. The priest, who was conducting high mass, wore a black cassock, and the soldiers who were helping him with the service were in their uniforms. Two candles burned on the partially demolished altar on which a wooden cross had replaced the more ornate cross that had probably been removed to a place of safety. Although I could understand very little of the service, I must say that I was very much impressed with the performance. The singing especially was impressive.

I left for 232 at about four in the

Church at Bethincourt. Notice the clock hanging in the steeple, Christmas 1917.

afternoon and was enthusiastically received by Meadowcroft who was anxious to get back and consume his share of the Christmas dinner. I had brought along some cigarettes and other good things that I had received in the box and passed them around to the Frenchmen who were very grateful. We had been issued an extra liter of *pinard* that day, so after the usual supper of soup and boiled cabbage, which I cared nothing for after our real Xmas dinner, the evening passed quickly and enjoyably. Things were unusually quiet that night, the Germans having evidently decided to lay off for the day, so I did not have a single call all that night, for which I was really thankful. I finally got tired of bickering with the French, so I crawled into one of the bunks, and amid the clattering of the rats on the tin roof overhead, at last dropped off to sleep. Such was my first Christmas away from home.

Most of the boxes have arrived, but there are one or two that have not as yet reached me. I surely am thankful to all my friends who were so thoughtful in remembering me. The receipt of the boxes was the one bright spot in what was otherwise a very drab and unusual Christmas. It is needless to tell you of how I missed you all, and I hope that I will soon hear from you as to your enjoyment of the day.

Cemetery at Jouy-en-Argonne.

S. S. U. 643. Convois Auto
American Exped. Forces
Par B. C. M. Paris, France
December 29th

Dear Mother,

I wish you would take notice of my address. It is practically the same and you might put down in the corner of the envelope, formerly S.S.U. XXXI. This is our new address that is to be in force now that the American army has taken us over. We are receiving new orders almost every day. They are for the most part unnecessary and we all wish that the service had remained on its old basis and had not been interfered with by the U.S. Army. The most exasperating order of all is the one concerning our mail. We are now allowed only to write one letter of one page and a half a day. These letters are all to be read and censored by our own lieutenant. This we all consider an outrage. It is bad enough to be over here without further separating us from our friends at home by putting a restriction on our mail. I hate the idea of having one with whom I associate every day read my letters, and then the enforced shortness is also a rotten idea. But *c'est la guerre*. What I think of the whole organization, its officers and its restrictions, is not fit to be written.

I looked forward to telling you at length about my Xmas, but all I can say now is that we all passed a very pleasant day. As I was compelled to go on duty immediately after dinner and go out to post, I was able to participate in both a French and American celebration. Of course, I missed you all terribly and therefore did not get the same joy out of the day as in former years. I hope my absence was not felt too much and that you all enjoyed your festivities.

It pleases me immensely to acknowledge the receipt of package No. 2 and the package you sent from Canada. They arrived on the same day, December 26th. You must know how grateful I am for all those little remembrances. I never knew how numerous and thoughtful my friends were. If I am unable to send each a letter of appreciation, I wish you would express my extreme gratitude to them all for me. We are still up here but are reasonably sure of going *en repos* in the very near future. The weather is cold but not disagreeable, about six inches of snow on the ground. The ground is thoroughly frozen, which makes driving very good. The blanket of snow sort of takes the curse off of the appearance of things, especially the terribly mutilated countryside. I am still in good health, although several of the boys are suffering from colds and rheumatism. I have plenty of warm clothes and am contented with my lot. But oh! how I wish I was with you all again.

Résumé of the year 1917. June 27th – December 31st.

June 27th Left Buffalo

June 28th Arrive at New York after stopping off at Easton

June 30th Sailed from New York on S.S. "Touraine"

July 9th^h Arrived at Bordeaux and left same day for Paris

July 10th Arrive at Paris and proceed to 21 rue Raynourd

July 14th Leave Paris on Bastille Day—very disappointed

July 14th Arrive at May-en-Multien training camp

July 24th Leave May for Paris. New section # 31 formed

July 24th Arrive Paris and go to rue Raynourd

July 27th Leave Paris as the newest section

July 29th Arrive at Bar-le-Duc and stay at *parc*.

July 31st Arrive at Érize-la-Petite, leaving Bar same morning

August 11th Leave Érize having been attached to the 25th D.I.

August 11th Arrive at Ville-sur-Cousances, relieving S.S.U. 29

August 12th Arrive at Recicourt

August 18th Leave Recicourt

August 18th Arrive at Érize-la-Petite

September 15th Leave Érize, having been attached to the 14th D.I.

September 15th Arrive at Condé-en-Barrois

September 27th Enlisted in U.S. Army for duration of war

October 2nd Leave Condé for the Montzeville sector

October 2nd Arrive at Jouy-en-Argonne where we are quartered in the town and keep the cars on the hill. Posts served are: Montzeville, Hills 232 and 239, Marre, Chattencourt, Esne. Triage at Clair Chêne.

December 25th Christmas at Post 232

January 4th, 1918 Leave Jouy at last for Velaines.

Ligny-en-Barrois — January 4th

This is a town of about 5,000 inhabitants lying some fifteen kilometers south and east of Bar-le-Duc on the road to Nancy. On the afternoon of January 4th, 1918, I walked to this village from Velaines, where we were cantoned, a distance of some two kilometers. We entered the village through a gate which arches the main street of the town. We soon came upon a spacious square, around which the principal buildings were located. To the left lay the *hôtel de ville* or town hall. The town's hostelry, the *Hôtel Cheval Blanc*, faced this edifice on the other side of the square. Near the western portal stood the usual large church, probably fifteenth century, Gothic in style, numerous chapels off the sides and walls hung with a great number of oil paintings. Interspersed between these landmarks were the usual number of stores of sorts.

A typical French town: narrow, curved streets, here and there a mansion of some pretentiousness, a fairly large park, gloomy from an overgrowth of trees and not well kept up. On the right side of the town ran the double-track *chemin de fer*, and alongside of this, the canal winds its lazy waters from lock to lock. The river Barrois marks the opposite boundary. Along the river, driven by waterpower, are several large glass factories, which provide the principle industry of the town. The main attraction to me was the movie show. I was surprised to see "The Silent Menace," an American production, was running at the theatre.

I spent the night at the White Horse Tavern, the first time that I had slept between sheets in six months. The room was equipped with steam heat, luxury of luxuries. I decided that night that the war was all wrong. Shorty Mills, who shared the room with me, proved to be a very tranquil sleeping mate. I hated to climb out of bed in the morning, but it was necessary to get back to roll-call at 8:00. We really shouldn't have gone to Ligny as we had not secured permission, so when we did report we had to pay the penalty of cutting wood for the kitchen. Didn't mind this as it was terribly cold and it gave us a chance to work up a sweat.

I forgot to say that the town shows no effects of the war. Of course, the streets are filled with soldiers and there are very few civilians. I saw a man with a derby hat. He looked terribly fancy. I might add here that we are probably *en route* for Alsace, having left Jouy-en-Argonne on the third of January. Time will tell whether or not our guess as to our destination is correct. I should not forget to note that the village is in the midst of a very fertile valley, which spreads for about a mile on either side of the river. Quite high hills rise on each side of the valley, through which little roads wind their way to the smaller villages nestled in the foothills.

Velaines – Sunday January 6th, 1918

Received your letter No. 30, written December 6th, this morning. Glad to announce receipt of packages 1, 2, and 4. Hope to receive No. 3 in the near future. Thank you for making your letter long. Tell Red that if he ever comes over here that he is a bigger fool than I thought he was. Glad you got the letter that I sent to you through Ed Mueller. Also, pleased to hear that you received my Xmas cable. Had to send it early or not at all. Received the money. Thanks one thousand times. Are you sure that you can spare it?

So patriotic Jack Baker has arrived home. Great fellow. Still, I can't blame him very much. I certainly would like to get back home again, even for a short time. You will be glad

Cable sent December 8th, 1917.

to hear that I have plenty of warm clothes. And we sure do need them. We have struck the coldest spell of weather this winter. It has been zero and under for the past week and it doesn't promise to get any warmer. We had hoped that we would be ordered further south, but this seems to be out now. Started to receive government clothes and pay but both are slow in coming. There is evidently a shortage of regulation tunics for they have issued to us the tunics that are worn by the Canadian troops. We are just as well pleased as they are much more comfortable, especially around the neck.

As to pay, it seems that we are to be paid about every three months. As a private, I receive thirty-three dollars a month. From this is deducted six dollars and forty cents a month to pay for a ten thousand dollar war risk insurance policy that I have made over to you. As the franc is now worth about 6.60 to the dollar, we receive about 147 francs a month, a tidy bit of money when compared with the five cents a day that we used to get in the French army. We have also received our new tags that we are to wear, two around our neck and the other around our wrist. My number is 10254, a low number, but I am disappointed in not getting one under 10,000. But the best part of the change of service is the fact that we are now allowed seventy cents a day for food. This makes it possible to have a very good table. While in the French army we were only allowed about thirty-five cents a day for food. We buy most from the French. It is Argentine beef and comes frozen so stiff that we have to let it sit a full day before it can be cut up.

Argentine beef at Rembercourt.

Potatoes, cabbage and bread are also purchased from the French commissary, but this leaves a nice balance to purchase fresh vegetables, cheeses, jams, butter, eggs and other delicacies in the towns behind the lines. Of course, we still get our rations of *pinard* and *vin ordinaire* from the French. We have gotten so used to this beverage by now that it will be hard to get along without it if they do decide to take it away as they may. We get sugar from whatever sources we are able. It is the scarcest article on our menu.

The packages were wonderful. I had to make another box to hold all the presents. Will do my best to thank each kind friend, but mail restrictions makes this a rather difficult matter. Glad that the picture of Spencer is coming. So, my mustache makes you laugh. Well, what will you think when you get my latest picture showing ARW sporting a healthy bunch of chin whiskers? Yes, they are red, but I think that they will have to be done away with as they seem to have become the favorite abiding place of numerous cooties.

Good news! Our division has at last gone back *en repos*. The 14th D.I. has received orders to go to the Vosges and we are evidently going along with them. We were relieved by S.S.U.4 on the morning of January third, and during that afternoon made our way south through Érize and Bar-le-Duc, finally stopping at the town of Velaines near Ligny-en-Barrois. No adequate provision had been made for our quarters so we all spent the night in our cars. As it was way below zero that night, you can imagine that we did not spend a very pleasant night. When I woke up in the morning, I found ice had accumulated on my beard, and there was a quarter of an inch of frost formed on the inside of the car by my breath. We are all hoping that we will not have to stay long here and that we will be sent south to a more pleasant climate for our much needed rest.

This is the best news I have been able to write in a long time. We have been up at the front now for three months lacking one day, and believe me, we are a some discontented bunch. It is customary to keep a section on active duty only about six weeks, and when you get a three months' stretch you get fed up with the discomforts for such a long time. It did seem good to get back to civilization once more. The civilians that we see look very funny, after seeing nothing but soldiers for such a long time. The town that we are cantoned in is rather small, but Ligny, a much larger town, is only two kilometers down the road. This is where this letter is written from.

Our officers were negligent about securing quarters for us, so when we arrived we had nothing but a dirty old barn to sleep in. It was so cold that after spending the first night in our cars, most of as felt we should look for more quarters. Some found them in private homes and others, myself included, hiked down to Ligny where we were able to get a room for eighty cents a day at the one hotel in the town, the *Hôtel Cheval Blanc* (the White Horse Tavern). That night, when I went to bed, I happened to remember that that was the first time I had slept between white sheets and on a spring mattress in a little over six months. The room even had steam heat and a wash basin. Well, I'm just telling you that I'm living like a king. It really doesn't seem possible to me now that I have been able to get along in such a primitive way. Here's hoping I won't have to take many more turns at it.

Savonnières – January 16th

I am writing this to you while enjoying the warmth and comfort of the Hotel de Gare in Bar-le-Duc. We moved from Velaines on the tenth of January and are now cantoned in much more comfortable quarters in the town of Savonnières, a suburb of Bar. It is still bitterly cold and so we spend as much of our time as possible in Bar. I have secured lodgings in a private house. The people are very nice old French people of the higher class, their home in fact being one of the nicest places in town. They have never before taken soldiers into their home, but being an American and presenting a fairly respectable appearance, they let me have a room. I also get my breakfast there in the morning, *cafe au lait*, toast, eggs and *confiture*, all for the sum of fifty cents a day. They even put hot bricks in my bed before I retire. The bed is a typical French bed. It has enormous feather mattresses, and you have to climb up a sort of ladder in order to get into it. When you finally do get in, you fairly are smothered, you sink down into it so far. They are very kind to me and are always asking questions about America. They have lost three boys in the war and the fourth is at present at the front.

Bar is quite full of American soldiers these days. They come from the vicinity of Gondrecourt, where the second American division is in winter training quarters. They all have weird tales to tell about the hardships that they have to endure. They evidently do not have sufficient warm clothing and even their food is very bad. They also complain about the strictness of discipline. The other night there was quite a serious riot between some Americans and the French Colonials who are stationed in this town. These Colonials are colored troops that the French recruit from their foreign provinces. Unlike Americans, the

French do not draw a color line, and so these colored troops are accepted by the French girls on the same basis as any other man. This gets under the Americans' skin, so much in fact that there is always trouble whenever the two mix. A couple of nights ago, some Americans were in one of the combination drinking and dancing places, when one of the Americans objected to a colonial's attention to one of the girls. This infuriated the colonial, all of whom are magnificent specimens, and he started after the American with a large knife. The American pulled out his forty-five and dropped him in his tracks. This started a riot that led to the killing of five and the wounding of several more. As a result, the Americans were excluded from the city and the place was closed. A few more incidences like this are apt to change the opinion that the French hold of the Americans. It must be admitted that the attitude of the average American soldier is one of extreme condescension, and as the French are a very proud and sensitive race, they are soon to sense this attitude, and resent it extremely.

I resent this attitude myself, knowing as I do from intimate contact with the French that they must be judged as any other people. After three years of this carnage, which the French have born unflinchingly, it must be realized that thousands upon thousands of the very finest of Frenchmen have been killed or so badly injured that they must be confined in hospitals. Only the very old men, in many cases much older then Dad, and the very new and young classes are left to carry on. Naturally, the American who comes over here as a common soldier is not going to meet the better classes of French, no more so than French

Anti-aircraft guns near Jouy-en-Argonne.

soldiers would be welcomed into the homes of our best families should they by any chance ever come over to America in such great numbers. The result is unfortunate, as the Americans must judge their French allies by the types that they come into contact with. These types, avaricious store keepers, harlots, low types of peasant soldiers, and the general riff-raff that follows an army, are certainly not representative Frenchmen and surely should not be accepted by Americans as typifying the true French gentleman. No more so than the French should judge the American people by the wild bunch of unthinking American soldiers who compose the mighty A.E.F.

This is getting to be a rather lengthy epistle, so I think that I will have to stop and hope that the censor does not delete too much of this as information that may be of interest to the Boches. Have not as yet received box number three. Hope that we stay here the rest of the winter or at least until I get a chance to go on permission.

Souilly – January 20th

Dear little brother,

I was so glad to receive your letter and hear all about you. I was very much interested in all you had to say and I did so appreciate your picture. I carry it with me all the time. I think I have told you that my little dog was stolen, but I have another now, and I call him Trick-Trick, a French name. He is not a puppy like the other but is very nice just the same. He is brown and white and he is a very good "ratter." That is why I got him. He digs right down into the ground for them and always comes up with one, shaking it in his mouth. I am afraid that I will have to give him away because the officers have passed a rule which prohibits the keeping of pets of any kind. They have passed so many rules that I wish they had never taken over our service.

I hope you will write soon as I do so enjoy your letters. Remember me to all your little friends and do your lessons well. Tell Mother that I have again moved up towards the lines and am doing evacuation work. Our headquarters is at Souilly.

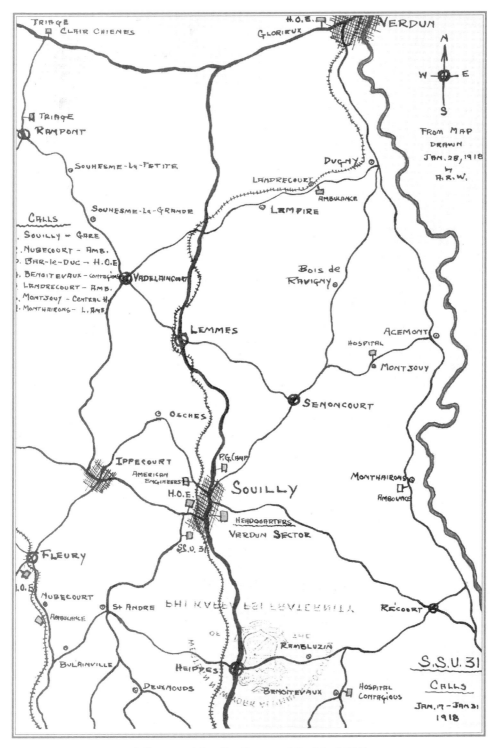

Calls around Souilly, January 17–31, 1917.

Souilly – January 20th

Dear Mother,

I received your letter number 31 the day before yesterday, making only two letters out of the last seven of eight that are missing. All of your letters contain some reference to the activities of Dad in his efforts to raise money for some sort of war fund. The papers, too, are all full of some sort of scheme to raise money ostensibly to be lavished on the boys over here. The more I read of these affairs the hotter I get. These funds are in the main part extravaganzas and frauds. To think that the people at home must be subjected to these continual drains is maddening. Our government has ample means to care for its boys. To facilitate these ends, they have imposed enormous taxes on everything taxable except the Senators themselves. With the money this raised they are more then capable of ministering to our comforts. The government showed they did not rely on this aid when they passed this enormous financial bill. Of course, I know that pressure is strong upon everyone to support these funds, but I think in the real part they are useless. I have not as yet seen one instance where we have benefited from them.

I am still very strong, although a number of the boys have and are suffering from colds and gripe due to extreme changes in the weather. Five days ago it was bitterly cold. Now it is so warm that we are going around in our shirt sleeves.

Contrary to all expectations, we have been suddenly moved back to active duty. This time we are cantoned in the village of Souilly, the headquarters of the Verdun front. We arrived here on the seventeenth and are rather comfortably quartered near the quarters of a

Carrier pigeon station, Souilly, 1917.

regiment of American engineers who are running the railroads in this sector. We are doing evacuation work entirely and although there is no danger in this type of work, the runs are long and our tricks of duty are rather tiresome. We are all disappointed, as we had expected to get a real long *repos* in a climate that would be more cheerful than this bleak, war-torn country. We needed the rest but *C'est is guerre*.

Souilly was a village of small importance before the war, but its location in the middle of the Verdun salient, approximately twenty miles from both here and Verdun on the ever Sacred Way, has made it one of the landmarks of the war. Here it was that General Petain directed the French forces who so successfully resisted the repeated attacks of the Crown Prince's forces against Verdun during the hectic days of the summer of 1916. From this little village issued the orders that sent the valiant French troops on their successful advance beyond Mort Homme and the village of Cumières in the hot days of August 1917, and Hill 344 in November of the same year, both of which engagements I took an active part in. Let us hope that these victories will influence the result of the spring attack of 1918, Souilly being the center of gigantic operations to repulse the expected Boche, and the pending French attacks at the time of this writing.

Souilly's rise to world importance has been rapid and spectacular. The General Staff has taken possession of the old and picturesque Marie. The fields to the left of the town, before the war one large swamp, are now the site of the "Eight Track," standard gauge railroad yard of the American managed and operated branch of the "R.R. d' Est." In conjunction with the yard is the large H.O.E. and P.G. Hospital, capable of providing for 2,000 wounded. On the northern edge of the town, the pavilions of three Escadrilles of fighting planes are pitched. It is interesting to note that six American pilots set forth on their daily patrols from this flying field.

The village, besides being the center of telephonic operations for the sector, is the base camp for all Boche prisoners captured in the Verdun Salient. Whether or not this move has been taken as additional protection for the Staff Officers is a matter of debate, but it seems to have worked, for after the Boche had bombarded the town by *avions*, and had killed numerous of their own men who were held in the prison camps located near the railroad yards, they have never bothered the town again. "Cheap protection," I call that!

The town itself is stretched out along "The Sacred Way." Like all other French towns, it boasts of a fine church which is prominently located on the brow of the hill, rising immediately behind the "Marie." Its lofty, towering steeple dominates the entire valley. The

Ed Kline, H. Kottman, and A.R. Wolfe at Souilly Airfield.

town is full of the hated *gendarmes*, who under the observing eye of the *état major*, keep the town in perfect order and are thoroughly strict in their enforcement of the liquor laws. A small number of the inhabitants have fled the town, but the majority prefer to risk the frequent bombings from the air, and profit from catering to the rather lucrative trade provided by the numerous officers and well-paid Americans who are quartered here.

Our calls take us over practically the whole of the Verdun Sector, from Bar-le-Duc to Glorieux at Verdun; from the H.O.E. at Fleury to the Contagious Hospital at Benoite-Vaux. We even hit the Meuse River on the right at Dugny, Les Monthairons and Ancemont. So you can see that our runs are liable to be long and tiresome. The Americans seem to have plenty of American tobacco, so we spend a lot of our leisure hours at their camp "bumming" as much as we can. They know how scarce tobacco is, so they ask prohibitive prices for it: ten Francs, or about two dollars, for a bag of Bull Durham tobacco.

Have not received package #3 as yet. I hope you have realized from my previous letters just how grateful I am over your efforts to make my Christmas a happy one. I shall try to write all those who had a part in the making of the boxes, but this one letter a day business makes it rather hard.

Souilly – January 25th

Dear Mrs. Pike,

My hardest task nowadays is to find suitable words to express my supreme appreciation to my friends in the States who have so generously provided me with the many little indispensable comforts of home. And to you, my dear friend, I feel indebted above all others. The wristlets which have kept my wrists warm on many a cold night and the cookies, the baking of which I know you must have had a part, were wonderful, and Oh! so appreciated. I can only attempt to thank you in words so I hope that it may not be many more months before I shall soon be with you once more and have the opportunity of personally thanking you.

Day follows day and still the war goes on. I sometimes wonder if it will ever end. Like all others, I have fallen into the rut of this monotonous existence. Breakfast, dinner, supper, bed with an occasional ride in the ambulance. How tired I am of it all. The arrival of the mail in the morning ends the day for us. If we get one letter the day takes on a brighter aspect. Our spirits rise as the number of letters increases. If we are lucky enough to hear from "the only girl" we call the day a success and spend the rest of the drawn-out hours in reading the letter over and over again. Such is our weary existence.

Of course, when we are at the front, it is an entirely different matter. I don't wish to be alarming, but it is true that our service is one of the most dangerous in the army. We have a great number of casualties in comparison with the number of men engaged in service than any other branch of the army. This is due, in the main, to the fact that our work takes us continuously over the roads leading to the front, which are almost continually under fire. The very nature of our work compels us to travel these roads under all conditions. The services that are privileged to "hoof it," such as the Infantry and the Artillery, have the valuable advantage of being in either trenches or dugouts during bombardments. In this way they are practically safe from everything except a direct hit. I mean by this that when a high explosive shell explodes, the shell fragments fly at terrific speed in all directions. These fragments have the power to kill for a range of about half a mile in all directions. However, if one can lay flat on the ground, or better still get below the surface of the ground, he is practically safe. There is also the additional advantage of hearing a shell approaching. It may seem strange, but one quickly learns to hear an approaching shell in time to take precautions against its arrival. You even learn to distinguish between *arrivés* and *départs*, or shells coming at you from the enemy lines and shells from your own guns on their way to the enemy lines. They are two different and distinct sounds, and once one learns to identify the two, one never forgets the difference.

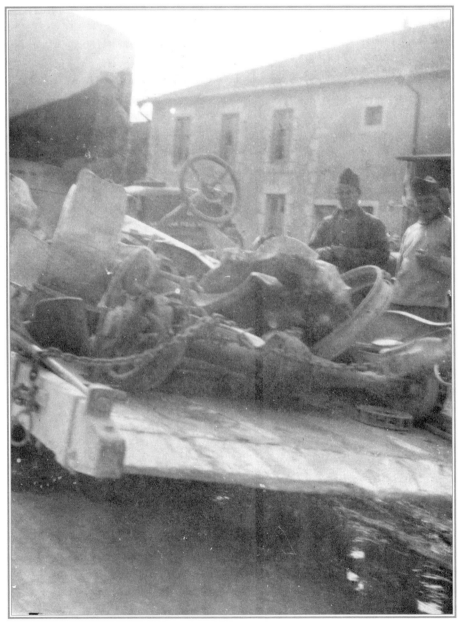

Ambulance after being hit by a shell. Schneider and Bingham are in the background.

You can readily see that being compelled to drive a car along a shell-swept road is a decided disadvantage. Sitting in your car, with no protection except your steel helmet, you become a target for pieces of every stray shell that may land in your vicinity. When an attack is launched, both sides do everything in their power to keep the roads leading to and serving the sector as impassable as possible. This is required by the necessity of preventing reinforcements of troops and ammunition from reaching the area under fire. Of course, the hotter the battle, the greater the casualties, and our job is to get these men out of the zone of fire. This can only be accomplished by making continuous trips through the barrage, until such a time as the wounded have been removed from the front to the safety of the evacuation hospitals in the rear.

We are also at a disadvantage during gas attacks. Of course, we all have gas masks, but if you have ever put one on you will realize how difficult it is to breathe with one in place. The best thing to do is to keep as quiet as possible so as not to bring your respiration above normal. In this way one can remain in a gassed area for an indefinite time or at least until the mask has worn out, which in the new French masks is three to four hours. We naturally have to keep moving and furthermore must drive our cars through the tangled messes of traffic that usually clog the roads during one of these gas attacks. To increase the difficulty of driving under these conditions, the lenses of the masks always become so clouded by the accumulation of moisture from one's breath that you soon find it impossible to see. The only alternative is to remove the mask and wipe off the lenses. This can only be accomplished by exposing yourself to whatever gas may be polluting the air. Therefore, it can be readily understood why so many of our drivers are almost constantly in the gas hospitals. You also can understand why all of us fear gas more than anything else and fairly tremble in our boots when we hear gas shells come popping into our vicinity.

The arrivals of gas shells are also distinguishable from high explosive shells. They make a dull "plop" as they hit the ground, in direct contrast to the terrific roar of the high explosives. It is funny how soon one learns to distinguish between these different shells, but still it must be admitted that it is pretty important that this should be the case.

In accordance with the decree of the ever-watchful censor, I must end my letter here. May this letter find you in the best of health and spirits, and may it convey to you my sincere feeling of gratitude over your many kindnesses.

<h1 style="text-align:center">Souilly – January 28th</h1>

Dear Mother,

I received letter number 33 yesterday, number 32 has not arrived. I don't believe I ever received a more wonderful letter than yours of Christmas Eve. I can not describe my feelings as I read it, but you may be sure I appreciate a little how you missed me.

I have some news for you. The ten new men we have been expecting for so long a time arrived last Monday, the 21st, night. This event will make possible the permission that has been coming to us for so long a time. Three of the boys have already started on their two weeks' leave; I, being the last on the list, will probably go about the last of February. I have changed my plans a bit and now intend to go to Corsica instead of Nice. The money that Dad sent me will come in very handy.

The ten men are members of the United States Ambulance Service who were recruited mostly from the colleges, and who received their training in the States at Allentown, PA., before being sent over here. These men were used mainly to fill in the gaps of the old Ambulance Service, but in a few cases complete new sections were organized equipped with one-ton white ambulances and sent out to the front to serve the American forces. Here are the names of some of the ten:

Kline, Edgar L.	Easton, Pa.	Lafayette
Kittman, John H.	Maplewood, N.J.	Lafayette
Kressler, Kenneth F.	Easton, Pa.	Lafayette
McInery, John E.	New York	Lafayette
Dickson, Donald G.	New York	Lafayette
Magnus, Albert	Chicago, Illinois	
McWilliams, William J.	New York	
Love, James S.	New York	
Cowan, Stafford G.	New York	
Kendrick, Percy O.	New York	

The best part of it all is that five of the new men are from Lafayette. You can imagine how glad I was to see them. They left the States only a little while ago, so they had news of a lot of the fellows that I had not heard from in so long a time. I understand from them that the college is fairly well depopulated. Practically all of my class has enlisted and many of the professors have also left. Warren Hamilton, my roommate, has enlisted in an artillery outfit and is over here now. I will surely have to get in touch with him if possible. Al Magnus, the new mechanic, is an old field serviceman who was in charge of the shop at the training camp at May-en-Multien. He is a peach of a fellow, as well as being the most energetic worker and one of the best mechanics that I have ever run across. He will do much to boost the morale of the section.

This is only a short note, but I will write you again before the week ends.

Typical road camouflage, Fort de Marre.

Souilly – January 29th

Dear Milton,

I want to thank you for your thoughtful effort to give me such a clear picture of your Christmas festivities. It seems from the large number of engagements you filled that you have become quite a "man about town." *C'est bien*, old boy, keep it up. I see the Old Amun Ra dances are still running true to form. Four hundred dollars is quite a little sum to be raised from a dance. They still must be flush with money in the States. Wish you had mentioned Ellen Lathrop in your letter. Don't you ever see her? I am glad you called on Marind. Any little thing you can do in that direction will be greatly appreciated by me. It displeases me to have you think that I would disapprove of your good times. We over here are not so narrow minded as to begrudge you your pleasures. We all realize that if we were home, we would be doing the same thing.

We have been enjoying a stretch of fine weather for the last two weeks. It is warm with plenty of sunshine during the daytime, and night driving is made a pleasure by a large, full moon and plenty of stars. That is, it would be a pleasure if it was not for the possibility of running into some Boche planes. On such bright nights they can see traffic along the roads and by flying low they are able to sweep the roads with machine gun fire. I ran across a couple the other night as I was returning from a trip to Bar-le-Duc. I could tell that they were near by the noise of the anti-aircraft guns. I stopped my car alongside of the road and listened. What a break! I had hardly stopped before I heard the roar of a plane overhead and the "whiz, whiz, whiz" of bullets all around me. I never moved so fast in all my life as I dove under the car and got below the engine. In a minute the danger was all over. I crawled out and inspected the car. Eight holes in the body and two in the back of the seat where I had been sitting.

Tomorrow we move again for the fourth time this month. It is *repos* again this time, at the Bois de Ravigny, on the road to Ancemont from Souilly. We will probably be up again very soon as this fine weather promises an early beginning of the spring activities. From all appearances, this is going to be the last big drive, the result of which will decide the war. I expect to be leaving for my permission around the first of March, and I am looking forward to this rest with a great deal of pleasure. I tell you what you can do to please me. Hit that Latin a little harder—not only for me, but for the folks. Anything that would please them is a favor to me. Give Spencer a dime for a soda on me and I will see that you get it back. Write again soon and love to all.

Search light used for anti-aircraft defense, Souilly.

Souilly — February 1st

Dear Dad,

 Although this is but the first of the month, the remembrance of your birthday coming on the 28th prompted me to write you my congratulations, so that they may come to your hands in due season. And with this remembrance comes others equally enjoyable; how the day before, Mother would make one of the matchless cocoa-nut cakes and other dainties, and how Red, Spencer and I used to clamor for the privilege of licking the frosting plate; then how anxious we would be to have you come home early, and when you did arrive and supper was finished: the "Big Surprise." I can see your face light up with delight as the cake was brought in, and also hear us kids hollering as the cake was cut, all demanding the biggest piece, after yours, of course.

　　　Although I shall not be with you this year, I hope my absence will not take away from the joy you will all derive from the day. I hope nothing but the best and most sincere of wishes for the day to send you, and these come from the bottom of my heart, being prompted by the deepest filial love and devotion. It is with the hope that the next year will find me home with you all to enjoy and participate in your next birthday that I leave you with the best wishes of the day.

Bois de Ravigny — February 3rd

Dear Mother,

Thirty-four and five arrived yesterday so full of news, and I enjoyed them so much. Package #3 also arrived a few days ago. I find myself very much handicapped in my attempts to write thank-you notes by this absence of addresses. You very thoughtfully stated in one of your letters that Miss Curtin's address was W. Delavan Avenue. For some unknown reason you left out the number. In order to get around the obstacles, I have written notes that I have placed in envelopes addressed to you with the idea that you will address the envelopes from home. I do hope the package containing Marind's picture will arrive safely.

We have moved again since I have last written. On the first of February, we packed up, and leaving Souilly, made our way northeast along the road to Dugny until we hit a large rest camp located in the Bois de Ravigny. This is a typical camp that one finds located in the various wooded areas throughout France, especially near the front. It is composed of numerous standard shacks, or barracks, some a hundred feet long and thirty feet wide, made of wood and containing bunks for about fifty men. They are hidden as much as possible under the trees in order to avoid their being spotted by enemy *avions*. They are used as rest places for the troops who are at the front. When a division is at the front, the whole division is never at the front at the same time. Part occupies the front trenches for about a week, and then they return to the rest camps, and are relieved by the other part of the division. So, they alternate while the division is at the front, the part at the rest camps always being in reserve in case that anything unusual turns up.

This makes the fourth change since the third of January. Looking back over the month, I find it full of varied and interesting experiences. From the first to the third of January we were at our old posts at the Montzeville sector. Moving on the third, we went about forty miles back into the country, to a little town of Velaines, where we spent six of the coldest days of the year. Retracing our steps, we arrived at the town of Savonnières, in the suburbs of Bar-le-Duc, where we enjoyed a week full of good times, settled in warm and comfortable quarters. After a week here, we moved again, on the seventeenth, to the village of Souilly, this time to do evacuation work for the Army. Here in comfortable quarters we stayed another ten days or so, enjoying the work and having the advantage of being cantoned quite near the quarters of a company of American engineers, who were running the *chemin de fer* in the sector. Then, on the first of February, we moved again to this cantonment. Such is our life of varied moves.

The next thing to look forward to is the Spring Attack. We hear almost every day that the first of the Americans will finally take over a sector of the front for the first time. They have been in training all the winter and are at last expected to take a definite part in the next attack. We also hear that there is a great deal of friction between the French General Staff and the American Headquarters over the policy of employing the American troops. It seems that Pershing insists upon keeping the Americans intact, with the idea of forming a complete American Army, and taking over a complete sector. The French and the other Allies, on the other hand, seem to feel that the best way to employ the American troops is to treat them as reinforcements for the various Allied divisions that are already operating at the front. It will be interesting to see how this difference will come out. Personally, I think that Pershing is right on insisting on keeping the Americans intact, and making preparations to operate as a complete American Army unit.

The arrival of the fellows from college has done so much to make my life happier. You cannot imagine how wonderful it is to sit around the stove and live over again the good times we enjoyed at college. It seems that we never reach an end, one recollection leads to another, and they have such interesting news as to the fate of most of the boys.

I am still in good health and the best of spirits. Hope that this finds you the same and that I hear from you soon.

Bois de Ravigny – February 8th

Dear Folks,

I have been very, very busy and find myself quite fatigued at the end of the week. I have practically finished the complete overhauling of my machine. It was quite a job and I am glad it is over. The whole car was taken apart and put together again. It is practically a new car now and runs like a sewing machine. It is a matter of self-protection for a driver to keep his car in the best condition. It would be unhealthy for one to break down on some of the roads between the posts and the front. These trips must be no stop trips, that is if you do not want to be compelled to get an entirely new car.

We are still *en repos* but it is rumored that we will go up in a short time. Getting terribly tired of this life. If I could only get home and see you all, even for only one day. I would then be glad to come back over here and enter this life again with my usual enthusiasm. But here I am over here now for over eight months, practically isolated in a strange country, amid strange tongues and faces, with no variation to the dull monotony of this dreary life. I am getting restless; restless beyond control.

At first, the new surroundings and the drastic change from my former quiet life made me feel enthusiastic for this new adventure, but soon the monotony of it all began to have a deadening effect on me. Now I seem to be living without a worry. Even the dangers that confront us have lost their zest. We have become philosophical about it all, realizing that we have no longer any command over our destinies, are in fact, mere pawns in a game of such gigantic proportions that we as individuals count no more than so many horses, guns or bullets. In this drugged condition, we seem to be living without a worry. It isn't natural. Even the poundings of the guns and the material noises that at first used to make me jump and take an interest in things, have become a commonplace thing. It seems as though my greatest and only worry is that my car will not run right.

I do hope that we will go up soon and have some real hot work like we had in August. Probably that will change things and give us a new interest in life. Anything but this deadly monotony. This army life becomes tedious to one who has been used to doing things. Everything is provided for the men, even brains. You become one ever so small, a part of a stupendous machine. Nothing counts but the ability to obey commands. Of course, that is as it should be. Without this unity and harmony of movement, the machine would be useless. But it is very, very trying on me. I do hope that it will not last long.

This may seem to you a very discontented spirit for a soldier of the U.S. to have, but I assure you that it is just a momentary spell that will soon pass, as have thousands of others. I have no reason to complain—good health, good eats and good quarters. Everything is fine, but do let me hear from you soon.

Bois de Ravigny – February 17th

Dear Mother,

Another week has passed. The days go slow, but the weeks and the months seem to fly. We are still *en repos*. Nothing happens to relieve the monotony. The nights are clear with *"beaucoup d'étoilles et une grande lune."* How do you like my French? This of course, means aviators friendly and hostile. The dull roar of the engines is almost always overhead. An accustomed ear can distinguish between the Boche and the French by the noise of the motors. The French are steady and rather high pitched, but the Boche are lower pitched and throbbing.

Both fly so low that it is necessary to take every precaution to keep lights from showing. Occasionally a dull roar and the shaking of the earth and the barracks tell us that the Germans have dropped a torpedo. We all hope that they won't drop one of their calling cards on our little settlement, nested as it is in the middle of a wooded valley protected by large trees that tower high overhead.

I haven't very much to tell you. I am as well as ever and contented. My permission will come pretty soon, and I will be darned glad when it does arrive. Remember me to everyone and love to all.

Bois de Ravigny – February 24th

Dear Mother,

I have had a very lucky week. Received two of your letters, but I notice that the two before them have been probably lost. Are many of my letters missing? I have found a way in which to elude my lieutenant as a censor and also the necessitated shortness of my letters. I have found out that we are allowed to send a few letters of sensible length to the base censor. We enclose them in a large blue envelope, which is sealed and cannot be molested by our lieutenant. This is ever so much better as I don't like the idea of having one with whom I come in such close contact each day having an insight into my personal letters.

Today being Sunday, the cook has promised us a feed. We have just finished peeling and paring three enormous pails of potatoes. These the *cuisinier* has promised to make, as only a Frenchman can, into *pomme-frites*, or French-fried potatoes. In addition, I have espied 10 large rabbits, a favorite dish over here. The French raise rabbits as we do chickens. Every farm house has its hares. We really eat very well now of late. You know that we have a new French cook.

The old cook, who came out with the section, proved to be quite unsatisfactory from the very first. He was always very antagonistic towards us boys, and in addition, we found that he was in the habit of selling our sugar, coffee and other scarce rations to the civilians. We finally persuaded the lieutenant to have him changed, and the new man has proven to be a dandy—one of the good natured fellows who never can do too much for a man. He has an agreeable voice, and he uses it to advantage, teaching us many of the catchy airs that are now holding sway in the Paris Bohemian cafés. He also has that smiling face, small black mustache curled up at the ends, shining black hair and neat, proficient air that we see in the cartoons and movies at home, and he does know how to cook. He was, before the war, a *chef de cuisine* at a grand hotel in Nice. Truly, we are lucky in acquiring him.

The fellows at the beginning of the alphabet have commenced to return from their permissions. My turn will come in about two weeks. I am ever so anxious to be off. All the boys are returning with such wonderful tales of Paris, Nice, Biarritz, Aix-les-Bains, and other brilliant watering places, that I can hardly wait to be off. I have decided on Nice, by way of Paris, Tours and Marseilles. Bud Lewis, who just came back yesterday, has generously given me a letter of introduction to certain English and French families of his acquaintance, who are at present spending the winter season in their *châteaux*.

It seems that Americans are feted extremely at the resort, so I am looking forward to an endless round of teas, auto and yacht rides, and happy parties like a trip to fairyland. Dreams of luxurious hours spent in viewing the beautiful *châteaux*, palaces, gardens and the fascinating life of the casinos of Nice and Monte Carlo, and even a trip now and then to the snow-capped Italian Alps, which rise abruptly from the blue stretch of the Mediterranean, fill me with expectations, and help me pass many of the loathsome days of *repos*.

It seems that Meadowcroft, who has just returned, had a rather unusual experience. The first day that he was in Paris, he ran across a poor French girl whose parents and family were in the part of France occupied by the Germans. He was so affected by her story that he generously gave her all of his vacation money. Then he had to spend the rest of his time in Paris, making enough to live on by drawing pictures, which he sold to passers-by. He slept on the benches along the Seine, and generally lived by his wits, but he had a grand time just the same.

I leave you in the best of health and spirits, my dear Mother, and with love to you all, I remain.

A.R.W. and Pierre at Ravigny.

Bois de Ravigny – February 29th

Dear Spencer,

Here it is, Father's Birthday, and I find myself writing to you to congratulate you on yours. You must be a great big lad by now. Let me see, how old are you now—eight or nine? I have really forgotten. You know, I always think of you as the little "duffer" who used to run around in overalls up at our little place on the beach. That is the way I like to think of you. That is why I was so glad to receive that picture of you.

I had just started to write this letter, when I heard some yells outside. Everybody jumped up and ran out to see what was the matter. We were surprised to see our lieutenant standing down the road apiece, looking mournfully at one of the cars that lay on its side in the ditch. As we ran towards the car, one of the Frenchmen, who is attached to the section, emerged from the wreckage with a rather sheepish expression on his face.

This is the story: It seems that the French have given up all their expensive cars and have issued a general order that in the future all cars used by officers will be American Ford touring cars. Naturally, all members of the Automobile Service must learn to drive Fords, so they have been receiving lessons from the members of the section. They have not proven very apt pupils, really surprisingly dumb. Finally, Battershell decided that he would take a hand at teaching the men. So, that morning he had taken one of the men, and they had started out. Everything went fine until it was necessary to turn around. When the Frog started to back up, he lost his head and forgot to take his foot off the reverse petal. Battershell felt the car going backwards, so he jumped out just in time to see the old bus tumble over into the ditch, Frog and all. Nobody was hurt, and when the bunch got together, they righted the car and lifted it back on the road, surprisingly none the worse for wear.

Haven't very much to tell you. We are still *en repos* in this rather quiet part of the country. There seems to be quite a good deal of munitions and other supplies moving up to the front. Everywhere we run across rumors of the expected spring drive. We were rather disappointed about the reports about how the Germans had driven through the Italians on the Italian front. It was necessary for the French to send some of their best troops down there to stop the advance. The French are very bitter about the outcome of the Italian Campaign, and do not hesitate to call the Italians every sort of coward and *ambuscade*.

I hope you enjoy the good birthday cake Mother is sure to make you, and remember me by eating an extra large piece. That won't be hard, will it?

Part 4

Spring 1918

Introduction

The spring of 1918 brought new hope for a decisive, victorious campaign, although hope was tinged with a sense of dread that the Allied soldier was nearing the end of his ability to persevere. Wolfe's long-delayed permission (furlough) finally arrived; he journeyed to Aix-les-Bains rather than his choice of Nice.

Throughout Royce Wolfe's service in France he encountered members of his old college fraternity, providing instant comradeship, a link to home, and a sense of belonging to a greater community.

Bois de Ravigny – March 1st

I am writing you on Friday this week instead of on Sunday because the ever-changing rules have decreed that only one letter shall be sent on Sunday. I have written Spencer a birthday letter, and I do hope he has an enjoyable day.

As the time for my permission approaches, I want to tell you of some of my plans. I have collected numerous souvenirs and other things that will be of interest. I intend to take them to Paris with me, where I understand I will be able to ship them home via the American Express. I do hope that they will arrive safely as I prize them very much. It is necessary for me to use this opportunity to get rid of them as the new regulations have cut us down to one duffel bag and one blanket roll.

This is a list of the articles in as far as I am able to tell right now, and I will also give you instructions as to the disposal of some of the articles.

1. Nose of a German 77 shell; this has been unloaded and is safe, but do not handle it too much.

2. Sign of the "Crown Prince Tunnel"; one of the three under Mort Homme, captured by the French in August.

3. Two small French 37 shells, used in trench mortars. These are also safe for handling.

4. Key to the opera house at Verdun, taken by me from the door of the partially destroyed building.

5. Stained glass from Verdun Cathedral; given to me by the guide who showed me through the edifice.

6. Three French sabers and one German saber which I have collected from the numerous equipment dumps.

7. Two watercolors by a French friend of mine who does some really remarkable work. Give one to Marind.

8. Two French shells (75mm) which have been engraved and fashioned by one of the Frenchmen.

9. Two paper knives which I made out of regular bullets, and which you can give to anyone you wish.

10. One German helmet and a skull that I picked up while on a trip up to Mort Homme to the left of Verdun.

There will probably be a lot of other things which I will tell you about later. The box will probably come through Canada, and you will have to go across the ferry for it. Let me know of its arrival immediately as I am naturally anxious that it gets to you safely. I haven't heard from you in the last ten days. Also, all packages from #5 on are still missing. I am in the best of health and expect to leave for Nice in about ten days. Can hardly wait until the time comes.

Group of trophies sent home, March 1918.

Bois de Ravigny – March 8th

Dear Mother,

As I may now be leaving any day for Nice I thought I would write now as it may be difficult to write *en route*. We are still *en repos*, Mother, and prospects of getting into action in the immediate future seem vague. It would not surprise me to find the section still idling when I return from permission. We are inclined to lay this long period of inactivity to the French lieutenant, who has shown himself distinctly antagonistic to the Americans in the section. It is rumored that, through his drag with the D.S.A., he has requested that the section remain dormant as long as possible. We are all displeased with this attitude. There is no reason for such a request. The cars were never in such good condition, the fellows never so keen for action, and the general condition of the section has never been so good as it is at present. We all suspect that the French lieutenant is doing this as a matter of spite because of the animosity that has existed between himself and the fellows, which has been very acute of late. He has been the section's one detriment since it left Paris. Our best attempts to get rid of him have been to no avail.

I ran across some American peanut and popcorn venders the other day. It seemed so strange to run into their unusual lingo so far from home. They are members of one of the disgraced Italian regiments who have been sent to the French and English fronts to dig trenches, repair roads and do other menial work because of their traitorous retreat before the Germans. Three of them lived in New York, and another had lived in Boston. I felt sorry for the poor fellows because the pompous little Frenchmen treat them with even greater contempt than their Boche prisoners.

I was quite startled the other day by the amazing facts concerning Japan which were contained in a letter that one of the fellows received from a friend of his who is teaching in Japan. You have probably read about and pondered over the relations between Japan and our country during the last decade. I have always distrusted their intentions, and even the coming of Viscount Ishii with his mission left me cold. I felt strongly that this sending of a mission was a diplomatic gesture to deceive the American populace as to the true intent of the Japanese policy. The letter that I referred to has given grounds to my worst fears. To quote in brief:

"I believe that Ishii is sincere when he says that the aims and ideals of America and

Japan coincide, but he is affected by that arrogant bombast and blind self-conceit that all the Japanese people have in a greater or lesser degree. The facts are entirely different from what he in his smooth way would have us believe."

Have the papers at home mentioned that Japan is going into Shantung, the province about Tsingtao, Northern China, and setting up a civil government? Have Japan's peace proposals, in which she demands, as of yet unofficially, the right to keep the colonies she captured from Germany, been brought to light as yet? Have you heard about the underhanded way in which Japan is supporting the northern faction of China, thereby prolonging the dissention there, because, as one of her college professors said in a recent article, "A highly developed and united China is a consistent menace to the future of the Japanese empire."

". . . Even here, in Osaka city, the Pittsburg of Japan, we hear about these things only in hushed tones, from the friends of China or from the occasional reports of a fearless daily. They serve to explain the hate and fear of all China, including her foreign residents, for Japan, the Eastern Menace, and tell the whole world that Japan is following the German ideal in her international relations."

The writer then goes on to give specific and appalling instances of the drastic measures that the imperialistic government is taking to forward her policy of Oriental supremacy. The majority of the government officials oppose the spread of Christianity as a breeder of democracy, the peril of the Japanese officialdom. Christian editors are being continually persecuted because they have fearlessly attempted to make known the existing conditions.

He also shows how pathetic and useless have been Japan's attempts to introduce modern industry and modes of living, but he points out that the Japanese are probably the most ambitious people on Earth, and that although they do not at once seem ready to adapt themselves to Western ideas, it is to be expected that their usual persistence and perseverance will eventually overcome what obstacles seem to obstruct their path to modernization. He predicts that the near future will find a straightened and imperialistic Japan in the role of Germany, as the world's most serious menace to peace.

This is indeed a question of vast importance. I feel that the European war has only put to one side for a few years the facing of the fact that the situation existing between our country and Japan is very serious and will eventually have to come up for serious consideration. I hope that the Allies will not have to call upon the Japanese for assistance to any great extent, for in that way we will be playing into their hands and increasing the already exalted opinion that they have of their own importance. So, it would seem that the east is producing questions as grave as the ones the countries of the west are now trying to solve. I send you all the deepest of love.

Bois de Ravigny – March 9th

Dear Dad,

It really pays to wait a long time to hear from you because when they do arrive, your letters are such wonders. I have never received a more flattering letter in all my life. I am sure that I am not worthy of your change of opinion as yet, but believe me, a letter like yours kind of backs me up, and makes me resolve to try more than ever to be worthy of such an opinion.

Sorry to hear about the strained business situation. Makes me think that you at home are being subjected to more hardships than we over here. This is a fine spring day, and we have just completed our Saturday morning inspection of persons and barracks. A good idea, as you know the fellows are inclined to become mighty slack as to personal appearance, and the barracks accumulate a surprising amount of rubbish during the course of a week, so we are all compelled to be cleaned and shaved at least once a week. The thought occurred to me the other day that some of the people at home, who have been so kind to write to me, have not as yet received my answer. I want to assure you and have you inform my friends that I have been most conscientious in my attempts to answer letters. If anyone has failed to hear from me it is because the letter has been lost in transit, as so often happens. I have answered every letter I have ever received.

Summer begins officially today. We have been instructed, as have all people living in France, to set our watches ahead one hour. In this way it is figured that there will be one more hour of daylight at the end of the day, which will be of more use than having it wasted by sleeping in the morning. It is called "The Daylight Saving Scheme," and so tomorrow I will be getting up at 7:00 instead of 8:00. The idea seems to be rather practical.

SONG OF THE AMBULANCIER

WE CAME TO FRANCE, TO DRIVE AN AMBULANCE,
AND NOT TO PUSH A TRUCK OF SHOVEL S___ FOR FRANCE,
P.I. SAID, 'GOD DAMN YOU AMBUSCADES',
YOU'VE GOT TO WORK FOR FRANCE IN A THOUSAND DIFFERENT WAYS.

WE WENT TO MAY, AND THEN TO BOUVAISE,
WHERE WE LEARNED TO DRIVE THE BERLIOT,
TOUT SWEET CHOCOLATE, QUACK - QUACK OMELET,
WE NEVER USED TO DO LIKE THIS BEFORE.

WE'VE GOT A NEW LIEUT, WHO DRINKS LIKE HELL,
BUT WHEN HE HEARS AN OBUS, HE DON'T SHOW UP SO WELL.
HE SCURRIES BACK TO CAMP IN HIS OLD STAFF CAR
AND HAS A LITTLE DRINK AT HIS PRIVATE BAR.

SO HERE'S A TOAST TO 633,
THE GOD-DAMDEST CONDUCTURES, THAT EVER CLIMBED A TREE,
THEY BREAK ALL THEIR RADIATORS, LOSE ALL THEIR TOOLS,
BUT WHEN IT COMES TO GET SOME PLACE, THEY ALL DRIVE LIKE FOOLS.

THREE YEARS MORE, THREE YEARS MORE,
THREE YEARS MORE OF THIS GOD DAMN WAR,
WE'LL HOIST OLD GLORY TO THE OLD FLAG POLE,
AND WE'LL ALL REINLIST, IN A PIGS A___ HOLE.

RESEMBLEMENT, GUARDEZ-VOUS,
EN EVANT MARCHE LIKE THE FRENCHMEN DO
UN, DUO, TROIS, QUARTE, WHAT THE HELL DO YOU THINK OF THAT.
WE NEVER USED TO DO LIKE THIS AT HOME.

A.R.W. - NOV. 1917

"Song of the Ambulancier"

Ever since America's declaration of war, the French soldier has been actively awaiting the time when the valiant Americans would take a definite part in the hostilities. The Americans, in fact, have been the one topic of conversation for months past. The French have heard wonderful tales of how the Americans were all sturdy six-footers, and have asked us over and over again if these reports as to their physiques were correct. Of course, we have answered in the affirmative. The result has been that the French have expected to lay eyes upon a group of giants when at last they were privileged to see the troops of the U.S. finally come into action.

This long anticipated event came to pass the other day when we least expected it. It was about the middle of the day, when most of us were sitting around the barracks enjoying an after-dinner smoke, that we heard some yelling from some Frenchmen down the road, and then one of them came running towards me saying excitedly: "The Americans are coming! The Americans are coming!" Thrilled at the prospect, but nevertheless unable to believe that the Americans would be so rash as to march up the road in the middle of the day and in full sight of the Boche observation balloons, we ran down to the road. Sure enough, there in the distance a long line of khaki-clad soldiers were wearily treading along the road in columns of four.

The word had quickly spread through the camp that the Americans were coming, so when the head of the column finally drew abreast of our position the whole camp was eagerly watching from the sides of the road. It was great to see the Americans coming in, I admit, but every one of us, including the Frenchmen, was greatly disappointed. Instead of a mass of stalwart, smiling, well-built Americans, as we had visualized, we viewed, with astonished eyes, the most conglomerate, bedraggled, weary and forlorn looking soldiers that I have ever laid my eyes upon. To add to our astonishment, we found that they could not even talk English.

We finally found a real American lieutenant who explained the mystery. It seems that we were looking at a regiment of the regular army that had been recruited before the war. They were, the lieutenant explained, practically all foreign immigrants who had enlisted in the army in order to become citizens more quickly. He also stated that he was compelled to choose his non-coms for their ability to speak foreign languages as otherwise he would not be able to make himself understood. They had marched twenty miles that day with hundred-pound packs and were naturally all petered out. The lieutenant said that they had been in training all the winter and were moving up to take over a sector to our right. Well, you can imagine how disappointed we were, and how thoroughly disillusioned the Frenchmen were. We did our best to explain the situation, but nothing we could say could explain the presence of so many of the hated Italians and even more despised Greeks in the ranks of the vaunted Americans.

We spoke to the lieutenant about the fact that it was very unusual to make a relief in broad daylight, but he evidenced no cause for concern at this information. It would be interesting to hear what the French commander says when he sees the Americans come walking up the road.

I hope it will not be long before I hear from you again, and, in the meantime, I hope conditions at home will improve. I leave you in the best of health and morale.

Bois de Ravigny – March 10th

My Dear Mother,

I am writing an extra letter to you this week to tell you about a trip that I took the other day. I received permission to take a car and, with Shorty Mills, take a trip up to the city of Verdun, some ten miles from our camp. We had both been there many times before, but had never had time to see all the sights.

We drove up to the *Marie* in the center of the town and received the necessary pass,

Hotel cards picked up in the ruins of Verdun.

etc. Then we took our way leisurely around the town, peering into the deserted, half-destroyed homes, and in some instances rummaging around inside the houses. We found many interesting relics, and, finally, wound up at the Citadel. This, of course, was the most interesting part of the trip.

When I got back to the camp, I wrote down my impressions in a notebook I am keeping. Here they are:

Verdun—the key to Paris. How often the Boche have attempted to turn this key, and at what great losses have the French prevented these stubborn attempts. Now it promises that the key will never again be so closely menaced, but the Boche have left their curse on it forever. Never again can it be the same as of old. And what a beautiful city it must have been *avant la guerre,* commanding as it does the surrounding hills and the gentle valley of the Meuse River. What a happy, prosperous and contented life must have been the lot of its 45,000 inhabitants.

The city is built around the base of a fortified hill, the ancient citadel, whose stone walls tower to the height of over 200 feet. These massive walls are surrounded by an old moat. Entrance is gained by passing over the drawbridges and through tall gates. The whole

Place de la Cathédrale, Verdun.

hill is undermined by a labyrinth of tunnels capable of holding thousands of men, and at the time of this writing, filled high with munitions of all sorts. The date of "1836" is on one of the entrances.

The ascent to the top of the citadel is a long climb up endless steps. The top is about a half a mile in length and a quarter of a mile in width. This is the old city. Here, lining the crooked, narrow streets, are houses hundreds of years old, the Cathedral, the College Marguerite, spacious barracks and a large parade ground. But something more gripping attacks one's eye. It is the pitiful ruin that all this has been reduced to. Beautiful houses will present an intact front, but upon closer examination you will notice that the back of the house and its roof to be a total ruin. Some are completely demolished.

The goodly buildings of the College Marguerite, lying clustered around the Cathedral, are in some cases utterly destroyed. And the Cathedral, a wonderful, old, massive, impressive structure, after the style of the Cathedral at Rheims, but not so elaborate. A military pass, easily procured, is necessary to gain admittance. This restriction is to prevent the pernicious defacing of the edifice by people in search of souvenirs. In entering, the roof arches high overhead, but what does one see? Huge holes torn through the walls and the roof. The refuse has been cleared up now, and things are put in some semblance of order. Magnificent chapels are set picturesquely in the walls. The majority of the ornaments and pictures have been removed to places of safety. The chancel has not been hit as yet. In front of the altar is an immense, gilded portico, supported by four columns of dark marble, exquisitely carved in scrolls.

The soldier guide, who keeps a watchful eye on you, conducts you down a series of stairs to the right of the altar which leads to a small chapel. With the aid of a candle, the guide proudly exhibits the treasures of the chapel and shows the mural paintings on the walls, work over five hundred years old. I was given a piece of stained glass from one of the windows as I went out. From the vacant windows one looks over the low-lying country and the scarred hills beyond. The river Meuse flows sluggishly, a stream of verdant green at your feet. You look over the new town below, the destroyed theater, the railroad yards, the extensive park, the large barracks buildings across the river at the Faubourg Bevaux, and the crooked streets with their tumbling buildings. It is surely a decidedly impressive sight, one long to be remembered.

Such was my impression. One can not imagine the completeness with which this city has been destroyed. The country to the north, especially the hills that are the location of the famous forts of Verdun, are completely demolished. In the places of such towns as Bras and Fleury, that lie near the forts, not one thing remains that would indicate that thriving villages once were located there. Stretches that once boasted lovely forests are left with not one stick standing, not even a stump to show evidence of their former grandeur. The earth has been so continuously turned up by the exploding of countless shells that it resembles a vast dump heap. There is one valley near Douaumont called the Valley of Death, where during the offensive of 1916 so many men were killed and left to lay there, that if they were all resurrected., they would be so crowded that they would not be able to stand on their feet. Over 50,000 lie in this one spot. I hope that I have in some way conveyed to you the picture of this most famous spot.

Bois de Ravigny — March 14th

My Dear Mother,

I have become the victim of circumstance. Without a doubt, that stern lady of chance has found displeasure in me and as a result, my relished hopes of leaving on a long overdue vacation have been shot asunder.

Out of our dreams, in the middle of the night of March 10th, came her messenger in the form of our French lieutenant, who sadly awoke us with the news that as one of the boys, who had been evacuated to a hospital a few days ago, had contracted a slight case of diphtheria, we were to immediately pack up our necessary toilet articles and depart without delay to an internment hospital, there to remain in exile until examination should prove us free from dangerous bacilli.

Somewhat dazed over this unusual interruption to our tranquil life of *repos*, we descended to the *camion* which took us, quite a hilarious party by now, to a new hospital some distance away, where we finished our night's *repos* between white sheets and on the comfortable hospital cots. Here we remain and probably will continue to for the next four or five days.

This morning, when the doctor took our throat cultures, he remarked that everything looked fine. We will probably have to remain here only a few days more. It is really not so bad and I think that the only serious outcome will be the putting off of my permission. So don't worry, Mother, nothing serious at all. We are all a pretty healthy bunch of fellows after eight months of such life, and think it improbable that any of the old men will contract the ailment. The sick boy is one of the new fellows. He probably has not as yet become acclimated.

It turns out that the Americans have regretted their rashness in making daylight reliefs. They were spotted by the Boche balloons, and a road barrage was flung at them, resulting in several casualties. Furthermore, we learned that a large detachment was sent up the railroad to Dugny, where again they disembarked in broad daylight. The band was the first to get off the train and they immediately began to play. The Germans saw the proceedings and sent over a few well-placed shots that wiped out the band and sent the others scurrying for shelter. It's hard to tell the Americans anything, but they will soon learn from their sad experience that there are certain ways of doing things over here that they will have to follow whether or not they like it.

We are having a wonderful stretch of good weather and everything points to a rapid ending of this thing. I send my love to all and hope to hear from you soon.

Bois de Ravigny – March 17th – Saint Patrick's Day

My Dear Mother,

Well, we marched back to camp this afternoon in columns of four—25 whistling, singing, happy lads glad to be free from the confines of the hospital. The old barrack was quite changed and after the fellows had straightened out their belongings, the effect was a 100 percent better. The walls had been whitewashed, new and uniform stands for the stretchers had been installed, eating facilities had been improved, and things in general had taken on a more sanitary, pleasing, and orderly appearance. In fact it didn't look like the old place at all.

Every bit of this can be attributed to the amazing industry of our Sergeant Al Magnus. I have never run across a man like him. It is a common saying around camp that nobody has ever seen Magnus not working, and it is true. First up in the morning and last to bed at night, he works incessantly during the day. Lots of times I have heard Battershell chide him for not stopping his work and coming to his meals. It is entirely through his efforts that the section has improved to such an extent. Magnus hails from Chicago.

Things have been rather noisy up here as of late. As the French say, the Americans have turned on their guns and have forgotten how to turn them off. When there is no cause for activity, both the French and Germans have learned to conduct a very polite warfare. They send over a few shells at midnight and again just before daylight. The rest of the day is calm and peaceful; no reason why it shouldn't be. But with the advent of the Americans into the sector, everything is changed. They are continually firing their guns, like a child with a new plaything, with the result that the Germans think that there is something of importance going on, so they reply in kind. The result is very annoying to the French, who have learned from sad experience that while things are quiet, there is no reason to stir things up. They know that when a really important engagement comes along, there will be plenty of opportunity to fire off their guns.

Now for the good news: If the paymaster arrives tomorrow as expected, I am leaving for my permission. It surely has been long delayed, but will be nonetheless welcome. I still have that money which Dad so kindly sent, and believe me, it will come in handy. Things are in such circumstances over here that one needs at least 500 francs to have a normal good time. But I have even been able to save a great deal of my pay, so what I have ought to be sufficient.

You ought to see from this letter, Mother, that I am happy and contented, so it's all to the merry, love for all.

Going en repos.

Paris – March 19th

My Dear Mother,

I know that you will be pleased to learn that I have at last reached Paris, en route for Aix-les- Bains, where I will spend seven days. I left camp at Ravigny at 5:00 and was driven to Souilly, where I caught a train on the narrow gauge railroad, one similar to the dummy that runs to Fort Erie. After a tiresome ride of four and a half hours on a terrible road bed, I at last arrived at Bar-le-Duc too late to catch the evening train to Paris and with nothing to do but spend the night as best I could. After a great amount of searching, I finally found a room in the Hotel de la Gare. I had no more than got settled in bed when the landlord rapped on the door and wanted to know if I would share my bed with another American. It seems that accommodations were at a premium that night and rather than have the American sleep on the floor, he had suggested that I might be willing to share my bed with him. I told him that I would take a look at him, and so in a few moments a nice looking fellow came in from one of the American units which were stationed down towards Nancy.

He seemed agreeable enough and said that he had been all over the town looking for a room without success, and that if I would be so good as to put up with him for the night, that he would be willing to assume the complete cost of the room. He was soon in bed and as we lay there, indulging in the usual small talk, I happened to mention that I was from Buffalo. He then asked me if I knew a girl from there by the name of Hamil. Well, you just know that this fairly made me sit up in bed. It seems that he was an Amherst student and he had met Marind and Russies and all the bunch while at a dance at Northampton. Wasn't that a coincidence!

We were up rather early in the morning, and after having breakfast together we parted, he for his outfit and I for the station. I found that the next train did not leave until 10:00, so I decided to take a bath and change into cleaner clothes in Bar instead of waiting until I got to Paris. So I took myself to the *Bains Publics* and bought my ticket. For 50 centimes you receive a towel, a small piece of soap, and then you follow the attendant into one of the bathrooms where you find one of those old fashioned zinc bathtubs that are built into the wall. The attendant disappeared and soon returned with a couple of buckets of warm water. These he emptied carefully into the tub until, by careful measurement, there was exactly two inches of water on the bottom. In answer to my questions, he told me quite seriously that hot water was very scarce, and that he must be very careful of his supply.

I now have something dreadful to admit: this was my first real bath with hot water in over four months. In fact, this is the first time that I had taken off a heavy suit of underwear that I had put on when it first started to get cold. So you can imagine how dirty I was. I got into the tub and was soon horrified that the water was so dirty, that it seemed useless to wash anymore. So I got out my knife and fairly scraped the dirt off of me. Then I took the little towel and tried to wipe off the worst of it. The towel was soon so dirty that I could not use it, so I took the curtain that shaded the window and finished drying myself with it. Although dry, I decided that I was not clean enough to get into my clean clothes, so I dressed in my dirty ones again and left the tub room. Going again to the window, I bought another ticket, much to the surprise of the manager, and again went through the formula of getting prepared for a bath. This time I was satisfied that I was clean enough to get into my clean clothes, and so feeling several pounds lighter and very much refreshed in my clean uniform and under-things, I made my way to the station. The train came in on time and I was en route to Paris.

Paris — L'Arc de Triomphe du Carrousel.

Fortunately, I was able to secure a second class accommodation, which made the four hour run to Paris much more endurable. I met some Englishmen of the R.F.C. on the train and became quite frustrated over their attempt to convince me of the superiority of the English over the people of the U.S. They seemed to resent the fact that we did not declare war sooner, and were quite outspoken in their criticism of Pershing's plans for an independent American Army unit. They evidently had no use for the French, and no respect at all for their other allies. In fact, they got on my nerves, and I found their sentiments as hard to understand as their peculiar use of the English language. It was my first direct contact with the English, and I must say that I was greatly disappointed.

I arrived in Paris at 2:30 to find it raining *bien*. I was enraged over the impudent independence of the taxi drivers. After several vain attempts to secure a cab, an American nurse, who undoubtedly witnessed my failure, kindly offered to share her car with me. So, I finally got away from the *gare* and left my kind benefactress at the Automobile Headquarters, where I had to report for further instructions. Here it was that my usual hard luck came to the fore again in the shape of an order compelling all permissioners to go to Aix-les-Bains.

American Express receipt for souvenirs sent back to U.S.

So, my carefully-laid plans and expectations of going to Nice and the Riviera were completely shattered. I was ordered to leave Paris that evening at 8:00.

Before leaving the section I had secured a small French officer's trunk, about 12 by 12 by 24 inches, in which I had packed the numerous articles that I wished to send home to you. So, after leaving the Automobile Headquarters, I took this trunk down to the office of the American Express Company, near the Place de l'Opera. I found that by sending the trunk through England and Canada I could be reasonably sure that it would get through safely. This means that Dad will have to arrange to pick up the trunk at Fort Erie on the Canadian side. The cost of sending the trunk through was about ten dollars. This seemed a lot, but I thought that it would be well worthwhile, and it is the only way that I can possibly get it through to you. I hope that the contents of the box will be of interest to you, and as I have already sent you a description of the contents, I will not have to discuss it further.

This chore took a great deal of time to consummate, so it was not until the late afternoon that I was able to get up to the service club at Passy. I found no one there that I knew, so I took a taxi to the Y.M.C.A. Hotel. Here I ran into Doc Hagler, one of the section

Paris — La Madeleine.

men who was just returning from his permission, and we had supper together. Doc had been to Aix and reported that he had had a very good time. This made me feel much better.

While occupied in the consumption of some good old American food, my eyes, traveling aimlessly over the room, suddenly alighted on a familiar countenance. Sure enough it was Moff Ellis, a Phi Gam from college. I went over to his table and after mutual greetings of surprise and pleasure, we parted to finish our respective meals, agreeing to meet later in the lobby. It seemed so good to see Moff, and he was such an able persuader that I decided to take a chance and remain in Paris until the next day. So, we joined up with a number of other chaps from his outfit, Base Hospital # 5, and started out to enjoy the evening. We dropped into the Folies Bergère and were surprised to find that a few of the acts were in English, and that the orchestra played the latest American music. The place was full of soldiers, uniforms of every kind and description. I talked for a while with a young Canadian lieutenant from Niagara Falls, Ontario. He introduced me to a number of Australians—a great bunch of boys—all magnificent specimens, but cocky as the deuce.

We got back to the hotel well past midnight, but I thought that I would drop you a line before turning in, as I may not have a chance tomorrow. I will try to write regularly of my experiences, but cannot promise too much.

Aix-les-Bains – March 29th

My Dear Mother,

I am sorry not to have written to you before, but my days have been so full of good times that I found it rather difficult to do much writing. My leave is up today and I am leaving for Paris tonight on my way back to the section. I expect to spend Easter Sunday in Paris, that is if I arrive there per schedule.

I don't believe I have ever enjoyed such a wonderful time in all my life—one excursion after another to such interesting places and never a dull moment. I was fortunate to run across a number of Phi Kappa Psi men and have spent most of my time with them.

I have been staying at one of the best hotels in the town, the Hotel Albian, where such notables as Thomas Edison, J.P. Morgan, and members of the Royal Families of Italy and Russia have stayed in previous years. Just for fun I turned the hotel register back a few years and wrote my name under that of the famous Morgan.

Aix-les-Bains, as you know, is a very famous and fashionable watering place. It is situated in the middle of the French Alps, near the borders of both Italy and Switzerland, in the department of Savoie. It lies in a beautiful valley on the shores of Lac du Bourget, which mirrors the towering, snow-capped Alps that rise precipitously from its shores.

The Y.M.C.A. has taken over the magnificent casino as its headquarters, and here we enjoy nightly performances of vaudeville, opera, and moving pictures. The great gambling halls have been converted into lounging rooms, where one can read the latest magazines, play cards, and otherwise enjoy himself. The hostesses, all American girls, are doing a great job in arranging trips and picnics to the many and various places of interest in the vicinity. I have enjoyed a boat trip to the Abbey Hautecombe, a most interesting place, an auto trip over the mountain passes to Mount Blanc and Annecy, and numerous other bicycle and walking trips through the adjoining country.

But the best thing of all is the opportunity to again associate with American women. The casino is staffed by American women and girls who run the activities and

View of Aix from Coq. R.R. Hotel Albian in foreground

furnish a homely atmosphere that is priceless to us starved individuals who have for such a long time been deprived of the blessings of their companionship. I came over on the same boat with two of the girls, so we have had numerous good times together. I certainly hate to think of leaving, but guess that I have had my share of fun after all.

A.R.W. in front of casino in Aix.

Caserne Bevaux – April 4th

My Dear Mother,

My glorious vacation has ended and I am again back with my section. Feeling fine and fit and with greater determination than ever to see this thing through to the end. My pleasant experiences of the last two weeks have been a most welcome and essential break in the monotony of our existence over here. Those who plan our lives for us certainly must know their stuff because without these interludes of peace and happiness, most of us would go mad before the end of the year.

The trip back to the section was long and tedious due to the many delays and stopovers necessitated by an unusually large movement of troops and supplies. It took two days to make the ordinary run of 12 hours from Aix to Paris. I stopped over a day in Paris as it was Easter Sunday, and I wished to see how Parisians celebrated the festival. I strolled down the Boulevard des Capucines after a hearty American breakfast at the Y.M.C.A., and observed the crowds arrayed in their Easter finery strolling leisurely along the boulevard. It was quite a sight, and so to appreciate it the more I took a seat at one of the numerous sidewalk cafes that line the street and sipped a small cordial as I watched the passing parade.

Suddenly a strange sight took place. A terrific roar sounded down the boulevard, and jumping to my feet, I saw an immense cloud of smoke and debris issue from the building that housed the newspaper, Le Matin, just a block from where I was sitting. Instantly sirens started to whine their warning, and almost as if by magic the street that only a moment before had been alive with a gay throng was deserted. For some reason I did not immediately follow the throngs to places of safety but remained seated, fascinated by the strange occurrence. After a few moments another roar rendered the comparative stillness of the city, but this time the explosion was well away from where I was sitting. The explanation of this strange occurrence suddenly came to me: I remembered hearing on the trip up to Paris that the Germans had perfected a gun powerful enough to shell Paris. No one believed the story to be true, but here was mute evidence of the fact that the rumor was true indeed. It was a terrible blow to the morale of the French. Ten shells landed in the city that day, all but one being harmless. That one landed in an orphanage, killing six and wounding many more of the little inmates. The bombardment started a general exodus from the city on the part of all those civilians who could afford to get out. It was rumored that the government would move to Lyons. I haven't heard yet as to whether or not the bombardment continued—the papers are all surprisingly dumb on the subject.

When I reported to Headquarters I was surprised to hear that the section had moved up to the front the day after I left, March 19th. So instead of going back to Ravigny, I changed trains at Souilly and kept on until I reached the end of the line at Dugny. From here I caught a ride to Verdun and then crossed to the east side of the river, where the section was cantoned in the old military barracks called Caserne Bevaux. The buildings are in remarkable repair, affording us the cleanest, most comfortable quarters that we have as yet run across. The one disadvantage is that we are liable to be shelled out at any time the Boche sees it fit to do so, as the buildings lie within easy range of their larger guns, and they certainly afford a large enough target.

Still another surprise awaited me. During my absence our Lieutenant, C.C. Battershell, had been ordered in to Paris to take a course at some officers' school. He had

Faubourgs Belleview and Pavé, Verdun. Caserne Bevaux in foreground, River Meuse outlined by trees in background, and road to Bras and posts over hill-dotted lines.

been relieved by a chap who came over with one of the Allentown sections, Samuel S. Seward, a middle-aged man whose home is on the west coast. I believe that he was a professor or an instructor at one of the colleges on the coast. He seems to be a nice enough fellow, but a decided change from our free and easy Battershell.

The advent of this new lieutenant, fresh from the battlefields of the interior and the good old U.S.A., has introduced many new phrases of military life that as yet have been unknown to us. Inspections are very rigid, discipline has become something to observe, and army rules, regulations, and red tape have become firmly imbedded in our lives. There is a good deal of beefing about this new regime, especially among the older fellows, but I must say that the change appears to be for the best. Discipline, however distasteful, is very necessary for the maintaining of morale, and certainly the rigid inspections are for the best. Good old Bat was a swell guy, but hardly the leader that was necessary to cope with the personnel of the French Auto Headquarters. We all liked him, would have done anything for him, but in Sewell it would seem that the fellows have at least secured a representative and leader who is not afraid to make his own point—in spite of opposition from the French Bureau. Then too, the fellows seem to have more respect for the new lieutenant, as he has the necessary years. Let us hope that the new regime will bring forth better fruits.

Everyone seems most optimistic as to the outcome of the present activities. We all feel that this is the last enormous effort to settle things before we have the time and opportunity to set up a really formidable American Army organization. The Boche seem to sense the fact that if they are ever to break through it must need be before the Americans have the opportunity to perfect their plans. The total collapse of the Russians has helped them immeasurably, due to the fact that they can now concentrate all their force on the Western Front. Then too, we hear that thousands of Germans, who were captured in the early days of the war by the Russians, have now been released and these men will form the nucleus of the new storm troops that the Boche are preparing to make the last attempt to break through. But regardless of this unlooked-for aid and the collapse of the Italians, we all hold the opinion that their last attempt will be a failure and, that having shot their last shot, they will either give up entirely or withdraw to the Rhine, there to sue for the best possible terms of peace. I have a private hunch that it won't be long now.

The section, for a wonder, has been very comfortably quartered in these old barracks. The food still continues to be excellent, and the general conditions are very good. As someone said, "It's a hell of a war, but better than no war at all." We have all had some quite thrilling moments at the posts which we are serving. There are two of them and the work is quite severe at times. The weather continues fair enough, but quite a difference from the balmy breezes of good old Aix. I very fortunately met a chap named Shorty Major who was my *bon compagnon* on many a little party back at college. He is with one of the sections who are working the sector next of ours, and, as he is quartered in the same group of buildings, I see quite a good deal of him.

I found five of your letters awaiting me when I got back to the section. Also, so many others that I will have quite a time answering them all. Sorry that you have been misinformed about the packages. Only the first four of the nine have reached me. I have about given up hope for the rest of them. But I did receive the package containing Marind's picture. How did you like it? I thought it was great. Unhappily, the wonderfully heavy socks arrived just as I was wishing for some cotton socks. But they shan't be wasted never-the-less, as they will probably be handy for next winter. Hope that I will be home before that.

The nuts that Miss Yessir so kindly sent were deeply appreciated and I hope you will offer her my thanks as I may not be able to do it personally. I got the trunk of junk off by the American Express. Keep most of it, you know, except some of the smaller trinkets, but send the picture to Marind. I have my doubts as to whether or not it will all get through to you.

It will probably seem a long while since you last heard from me, but I assure you I have been quite busy, and that I will try to write more during the next few weeks to make up for it. I am in quite excellent condition except for a slight cold in the head which I contracted on the train.

Verdun – April 8th

Dear John,

Seemed awfully good to hear from you again, old man, and I must say I regretted extremely our somewhat mutual inability to reach each other before. Your letter brought me back with a bump to reminiscences of the great times we used to enjoy together; especially the last few days before I left. I will always remember that trip to Rochester with you and your mother.

My! How it did pour.

It seems a devilish long time since those happy days, and in fact it is practically a year now since I sailed. One year, fifty-two weeks, three hundred and sixty-five days. But as someone says, "The first seven years of war will be the hardest." Sometimes I feel that we will be enabled to test this theory. But I've got an optimistic hunch that the present offensive will result in peace negotiations of some sort, and it remains to be seen how many men the Germans will be able to sacrifice before the German people will recognize the hopelessness of their task and demand a peace at any terms.

It doesn't seem possible that the German people can be kept in ignorance of what a powerful combination the Allies are and how much more powerful they are becoming as time permits the Americans to get over here. From all reports, our boys are a bunch of fire-eaters. A Frenchman told me that the French don't enjoy having an American division near them as they make things so damnably hot in that sector. Judging from their sustained barrages, one would think they had turned their guns on and had forgotten how to turn them off. I have encountered a number of our regiments and I must say they are a tough bunch of men, in good health, morale and physique. I wouldn't enjoy being on the other side of No-Man's Land when a bunch of them go over the top.

I had a bully time on my permission and as they only come every four months, I am waiting for July to arrive as quickly as possible. I spent my seven days at Aix-les-Bains, a famous watering place in the Swiss-Franco Alps. I don't believe that I ever before enjoyed myself so thoroughly. It was one big picnic. I stayed at the best hotel, fine service, and excellent eats, spent my days in riding, motoring and boating, mountain climbing, playing golf and tennis. I visited many interesting places such as Mt. Blanc, L'Abbaye d' Hautecombe, Annecy, Chambéry, and Lac du Bourget. The evenings were occupied in attending plays and vaudeville acts at the Casino Theater. Believe me, it was blamed hard to leave when my week was up. But I would have given it all up for just one day, even one hour, at home.

Hope that this finds you in the best of health.

Verdun – April 13th

My Dear Mother,

I am taking this afternoon of enforced inactivity to relate to you my somewhat tardy account of my permission. As you will probably remember, I had made definite plans to spend my few days leave at Nice. But upon arrival at H.Q. office, I was informed that owing to new regulations, it would be necessary for me to make Aix-les-Bains my destination. This naturally was a great disappointment, especially as I had heard the most unpleasant rumors about this leave area. Rumor had it that the place was run accord to Y.M.C.A. standards, that the men were compelled to live in barracks under military regulations—in fact, life there included all that lack of freedom and individuality which I had so hoped to get away from for at least a few days. So, it was not in the most happy frame of mind that I boarded the 8:00 Express at the Gare de Lyon.

Fortunately, I was able to purchase a second class ticket and still more fortunately, was I able to secure a seat in one of the compartments, due to the courtesy of some English Tommies who were on their way to Egypt. The evening passed rather quickly as we all, through sheer fatigue, dropped off to sleep, one after another. I was very much amused by their queer cockney accents and their distorted opinions of America. I did not awake until the train came to an abrupt stop about 5:30 the next morning. Decidedly stiff from the awkwardness of my position but feeling a bit rested nevertheless, I stood up, arranged my mussed uniform, and stepped out of the compartment to fill my lungs with fresh air and incidentally take stock of my surroundings.

What a magnificent surprise greeted me. We were stationed in what appeared to be a junction lying in one of the most beautiful valleys that I had ever witnessed. A broad stretch of exceptionally level lowland spread as a great, soft green carpet before my eyes. Rising abruptly, at a distance of some ten or eleven miles, was a ridge of mountains, their towering, snow-clad peaks enshrouded with morning mist which gradually rose as the sun showed more and more of its glorious, flaming head over the horizon at my back. Turning, I noticed that the whole valley was apparently hemmed in by these rugged, lofty hills, except for a narrow opening, which faced the North and through which we had evidently made our entrance. The clear waters of a narrow winding stream seemed also to enter at this doorway to pursue its crooked course through the middle of the valley, and finally to disappear into the very foot of the ranges to the South.

At this point I was startled from my dreams by the shrill blast of a whistle, and the train gradually gaining speed curved its way along the western edge of the valley towards the tunnel which pierced the southern end. I had just one last fleeting glimpse of the valley as the sun burst forth in its full glory before we were engulfed by the blackness of the tunnel. The rest of the three hour trip was like a voyage through fairyland. Marvelously colored mountains supporting their snow-covered heads with dignity, little gems of lakes snuggled at their feet, and quaint old *châteaux* and castles perched upon such isolated promontories that many of them appeared to be floating upon the mist which hung suspended over the lakes. It was all too wonderful to describe.

Finally at about 10:00, we emerged from a tunnel upon a lake considerably larger than any of the former ones, Lac du Bourget, and our course ran along the very edge so close that the track was many times directly over the water at our right. The bank to our left was a steep precipice 800 feet high. We followed this novel course for some 15 minutes, then a sharp turn revealed to us a fair-sized little city whose white buildings, with their tiled roofs, covered a space of level land between the lake's edge and the foot of the mountains, about an eighth of a mile wide and a mile long. This, one of the Tommies informed me, was Aix-les- Bains, one of the most selective watering places in France, corresponding to our Virginia Hot Springs.

I had just finished gathering up my belongings and saying *adieu* to my English friends when the train came to a halt. Alighting, I found that my worst fears about the place were about to be realized. As it happened, I was the only American on the train, so I immediately found myself the sole prisoner of ten Y.M.C.A. men and at least seven M.P. They seemed as surprised as I was horrified at this reception, but one of them grabbed my grip and we started for the M.P. office where I was to register. I got through this performance without much trouble and I was then asked what sort of a hotel I preferred.

This was all wrong, according to rumor, but I came right through with a request for the best they had in town. As I was the only one, they complied with my request and after explaining that the rate for the eight days would be 149 Francs, they escorted me to the Hotel Albian. This I found later to be the best hotel in town, having entertained such personages as Thomas Edison, Pierpont Morgan, the royal families of Italy and Spain, countless dukes, lords, and scores of mere millionaires. It is situated in the center of the town on a rise of ground which affords one a wonderful panorama of the town, the lake beyond, and the mountains in the distance.

Someone must have been looking out of the window, because I had no more than

200 LAC DU BOURGET — Tunnel de Saint-Innocent
et Rochers de Brison. — LL.

Approaching Aix by railroad.

turned into the approach than the whole staff of the hotel turned out to greet me. One captured my valise and another my coat, the wide portals were held open by at least a dozen hands, and as I stepped into the lobby, the proprietor himself rushed forward with outstretched hands and led me to the bureau. Here I was relieved of my 149 francs, given a key, and after informing me that breakfast awaited my pleasure, was shown to the lift, which took me and my bags to the third floor and thence to my room.

What a room. The first thing that caught my eye was a bed topped by a three foot mattress with white sheets. I resolved then and there that little old Mr. Bed was going to see an awful lot of me during the next few days. I went to the window, after disposing of my baggage, and threw it wide open. Standing here, gazing on the wonderful picture thus produced, I was interrupted by the maid, asking to be directed as to how to draw the water for my bath, hot or cold. I found the water to be just the right temperature, and I must have soaked at least a good half hour before pangs of hunger reminded me that I hadn't had a bite to eat since dinner the night before.

So, attiring myself hastily, I descended to the dinning room where I ordered a real American breakfast: coffee, ham and eggs, buttered toast and jelly. What I did to that breakfast was a shame, and the bunch of acrobats who passed as waiters were quite astonished when I ordered a supplement of lamb chops and fried potatoes. Not knowing that I understood French, they remarked on the remarkable appetite of the Americans and one wit drew a laugh from his mates by remarking that if the Americans could fight as well as they ate, that the war would soon be over.

I left them still chuckling over their jobs and started from the hotel to spend the little while before lunch in exploring the town. My path led through the park—a beautiful little spot—filled for the most part with a rollicking bunch of children at play, with a sprinkling of convalescent soldiers idling away their time. Out of the park, I passed the ruins of the centuries old Roman Arch, the picturesque Hotel de Ville, and the other ancient landmarks that are centered around the central plaza. It is impossible to express my glorious feeling of contentment as I strolled through these quaint, narrow streets and alleys without a care in the world. It was very hard to realize that all of this was anything but a dream, and that I would be rudely awakened any moment by someone shaking my shoulder and telling me to get up and crank up my old *voiture* and proceed through the dismal night to post 232.

So, in somewhat of a daze, I wandered on. The gong announcing lunch had just commenced ringing as I finally turned into the hotel and made my way to the dining room.

15 **AIX-LES-BAINS.** — *Arc de Companus.* — LL.

Old Roman arch near public baths.

Verdun – April 23rd

My Dear Mother,

I think that I ended my last letter by saying that I arrived at the hotel in time for lunch, which was excellent soup, frogs' legs, mashed potatoes, roast beef, salad, fruit, coffee, and wine. During lunch I got into conversation with two chaps across the table from me who turned out to be fraternity brothers from Virginia University. They were fine chaps, and I spent the majority of my time with them and Dr. Hagler, the boy from my section who was staying at another hotel.

That same afternoon the four of us visited the Casino. This magnificent palace in the heart of the city had been taken over by the Y.M.C.A. as their headquarters, and thus all the privileges and comforts, such as billiard tables, lounging rooms, libraries, etc., were made available to the boys. The postal picture cards that I sent will give you a good ides of the beautiful gardens and grounds that surrounded the Casino, and will also give you some idea

Aix-les-Bains, Le Grand Cercle—the casino.

of what a wonderful building it was. The gambling equipment, of course, has all been removed and the large halls are given over to a theatre and dance hall.

After seeing the casino, we walked down to Lac du Bourget, where we hired a row boat and crossed to the opposite shore. We were all very tired when we got back to the hotel, as the lake is about a mile and a half wide, and we had not been doing much rowing up where we came from, although a boat would have come in handy in getting around some of those mud holes, now I come to think of it. We were also annoyed at the water blisters on our hands. These were particularly annoying, as our hands were just beginning to heal up. That was one thing that we all suffered from very much. In fooling around our cars and making repairs under difficult conditions, we were continually breaking the skin of our hands. Not having any means of keeping our wounds sterile, the result was that nearly all of us had swollen, pus-infected hands most of the time, the result of necessary neglect and forthcoming infection.

After another grand feed that evening, we all went over to the Casino where we enjoyed a fine moving picture. Back to the hotel after a brief pause at the Silver Grille room for a bit of a drink and then to bed. My, what luxury! Think of it. Clean white sheets after so many nights of nothing but a dirty, Le Galle-infested, *blesse* blanket. And the extreme pleasure of turning slowly, snuggling down into a feather mattress some two feet thick, after countless nights of tossing fitfully on a piece of stretched chicken wire covered with a thin layer of lousy barnyard straw.

After a most restful sleep, I arose rather early the next morning and, quickly dressing, made my way to the famous baths of Aix: natural hot water which has some curative power, so they say. Whether or not this is true, I certainly enjoyed myself and came out feeling refreshed and raring to go. Heading for the mountain side, I started the ascent, following a trail that finally emerged, after some three miles of stiff walking, at a little village high up on the side of the mountain, commanding a glorious view of the valley below, nestled at the side of the deep blue of Lac du Bourget—a fitting setting for the red-tiled roofs of the town of Aix itself.

I was very hungry by this time, so looking around for a place to appease my hunger, I spied a picturesque tavern up the road apiece. This hostelry, together with a church and about six houses, comprised the town. At the cafe I managed to get a very good omelet, coffee *au lait*, and some bread and cheese. This was served to me on a little terrace at the back of the inn, from where I could enjoy the beautiful panorama that spread at my feet. What a life of

Riley! I followed the main road down to the town and arrived somewhat late for lunch.

So that I may not draw this letter out to too great an extent, I will generalize to some degree. My mornings were generally the same—a bath at the Bains, a walk to some secluded tavern for a bit of breakfast, and back again to the hotel for lunch. The afternoons were usually occupied with walks, rides, and hikes to the numerous points of interest in the general vicinity of Aix.

I spent one very enjoyable day in motoring with Doc., Jack, and Tilley, to the foot of Mt.. Blanc, a trip of some 120 kilometers through the most wonderful scenery I have ever witnessed. The cost of the trip was not very great as we divided the cost four ways. The roads, especially the one that led from Chambery, over the pass to Annecy, were very dangerous, and at some places my heart fairly jumped out of my mouth. On two occasions,

33 AIX-LES-BAINS — Le Pont de l'Abime. — LL.

Picturesque bridge on road to Annecy from Aix.

the turns were so sharp that we were compelled to back up six times before we could get around in the De Dion Bouton that was carrying us. And there was absolutely no retaining wall or anything else to hold us if the brakes had not been working. Looking down into the valley, thousands of feet below, made us fairly tremble. But we came through without a mishap and certainly enjoyed the trip. The road through the Pass was so high that there were snow banks some 20 feet high still towering above us—even at that time of the year. Annecy, especially, was very picturesque.

Another trip of special interest was the one on the steamer that takes parties around Lac du Bourget, stopping on the way at the Abbey Hautecombe. The trip itself was very worthwhile, but the visit to the Abbey was quite an experience. The Abbey is built on a small piece of fairly level ground, not more than three acres in area, that lies at the foot of the precipitous mountains that rise along the north shore of the lake. The buildings are very old and gothic in architecture. There is a church and some buildings that house the monks; it is the only Abbey in all of France that is still being run by monks. This special concession to the Catholic Church was made because the Abbey really belongs to the Royal Family of Italy, several of the Dukes and Duchesses of Savoy being buried there. The grave of one of the

124   AIX-LES-BAINS. — *Abbaye d'Hautecombe.* — *Le Départ d'un Bateau.* — LL.   SELECTA

Abbaye d'Hautecombe.

Duchesses lying in the main isle of the church was especially interesting. It was a life-size statue of the Duches carved out of white marble—the most intricate carving that I have ever seen. We were also able to see one of the services. A bell somewhere up in the tower began to ring, and soon the monks started to file in. They were a funny looking bunch of men, and it sure was interesting to watch their service. One of the monks later took us around the buildings and showed us how they lived. They did not have many comforts, but they seemed to eat well, and for activity they made all their clothes and shoes and kept a little garden.

Other afternoons were spent in horseback riding, playing baseball, tennis, golf, and other outdoor activities. The movies were running almost continuously for those who liked this indoor sport. In the evenings there was always something doing. There was always some sort of a show at the Casino. One evening the Craig Players of Boston presented "Baby Mine." Another evening there were numerous vaudeville acts from the Alhambra Theatre of Paris. Elsie Janis won our hearts another night. Then there were several dances, in which the Y.M.C.A. girl entertainers took an awful beating. The dances were all run on the stag principle, that is, you could go up to any girl on the floor and ask her for a dance. The result was that all the girls were dancing almost continuously from 9–12:00, and with partners that stepped on their toes and sometimes even loitered there. But they were all good-sports and took it with a grin. One evening we spent in having a meeting and banquet of the Aix-les-Bains chapter of Phi Kappa Psi. Jack, Tilley, and I found some eight other brothers of our illustrious fraternity and we had a great reunion. If one is a member of a fraternity, he can always seem to find friends wherever he goes.

But the very best part of the entire experience was the opportunity afforded us to again associate with the American girls and women who were attached to the Y.M.C.A. These women had come over from the states at their own expense to run the canteen and conduct the activities in the various leave areas in the southern parts of France. They were really wonderful, and did everything in their power to make the boys feel that their short stay was like enjoying a picnic back home. They were going from morning to midnight, and how they stood it I do not know.

I was fortunate to find that two of the workers were on the same boat that I came over on—Mrs. Anderson and her daughter from Detroit. Having known them on the boat, they were especially nice to me and I must say that, due to their attentions, my stay at Aix was made 100 percent more enjoyable. I had several pleasant dinners with them at their hotel, and one afternoon they took me with them to call on some of their English friends who maintained a splendid home not far out of Aix. I met a Lord this and a Lady that, and was very much impressed.

I have yet to find a man who, having been isolated from all contact with the civilized world for an extensive period, does not experience a feeling of unparalleled contentment and pleasure upon being again afforded the privilege of conversing with a women he can respect—especially American women. We common soldiers, I realize, have little opportunity to meet or converse with the better class of French women, so those whom we do come into contact with are taken for what they are, or for what we think they are. The result is that, with few exceptions, we are not allowed that healthful contact with the right kind of the female sect that is so essential to our normal lives. The women of America will never be so thoroughly appreciated as when some of us fellows, who have had the opportunity of seeing the women of other countries, get home.

Well, this covers pretty completely my doings in Aix. Needless to say, I had the time of my life, and I sure did hate to take the train for Paris when my time was up at last. The trip to Paris was a terrible one, taking the best part of two days, including stops at Lyons and Dijon. This was made necessary by the great number of troop trains which were evidently on their way to the northern front. I stayed over a day in Paris, and then departed for Bar-le-Duc. I think that I have told you about this trip in detail in one of my earlier letters.

Scene of many a happy hour.

<h1 style="text-align:center">Verdun – April 30th</h1>

I hope that you have not been worrying over the absence of any news from your very prodigal son and of the scarcity of letters the last few days. I assure you that it has not been neglect on my part. An infected vaccination, which somehow or other refuses to clear up, and also an abscess on my right hand has temporarily put me out of condition. There is nothing to worry about, but I hope that the things will clear up in the near future as they are very annoying.

Yes, I realize that today is my birthday. Let me see, I am 20 years old and I don't feel much older than I did yesterday. But I must admit that it does seem as if plenty of water has gone over the dam since I celebrated my last birthday in Easton. Although time passes quite quickly over here, it does seem like a frightfully long time since I left you all less than a year ago. Can't help but wish that I could be with you today, if only for a few hours.

The boxes arrived over a week ago and how I did appreciate the contents. You have been very, very good in keeping me supplied with the many things that it is impossible to secure over here, and I am sure that you realize how grateful I am. As soon as I am able to handle my pen a little better, I will try to write my thanks to all my kind friends who have contributed to the boxes.

I hope that you received my letters telling all about my permission in Aix-les-Bains. It sure was a glorious time. I have noticed your references about Milton's ambitions to get into a camp. I suppose that if he is set upon it, that it would not do any harm. But I surely would make him promise not to get into any active service. One from a family is enough, and after all, there must be plenty of places where he could fit in without running the danger of endangering his health.

Kirk Meadowcroft, one of the original members of our section, is leaving this week. Friends have secured his transfer to the Intelligence Department where he will undoubtedly receive a commission. A very lucky fellow. We are all envious of his success in being transferred, although we all hate to see him go. Things are as usual. Quarters are unusually comfortable and, outside of the infections that I mentioned before, I am really in tiptop shape.

I used to be on fire with enthusiasm when I first arrived over here, but a year's experience of this sort of stuff will deaden any feeling. You sometimes wonder if anything is worthwhile. What is all the time, energy, and sacrifice availing us? I have been in this fog ever since my return from Aix. Don't know whether or not that little excursion into the past was a good thing for my morale. I am afraid that one comes back to this lousy life after such a wonderful time with a feeling of wonder as to whether or not the whole thing is worthwhile. What difference does it make, after all, whether the Allies or the Boche win, if the triumph is gained at such a tremendous sacrifice? Are those boys on the other side of the lines any worse or better, for that matter, than we are? Will the end, whatever it turns out to be, make conditions for us all any the better? I realize that this seems all to the bad,

Diploma conferred by French Government upon members of the American Field Service.

but I do get down in the dumps occasionally, especially since my run-in with the lieutenant. He continues to be very antagonistic and does not miss a trick to put me on the rack.

I have made an application for a transfer to another service, and hope that I will get the aviation. I told Sergeant Woolley to make the transfers to another section if he found that it would be impossible to get into another service at this time. Several of the other boys have made bids for a transfer, but Meadowcroft is the only one so far who has been successful.

Caserne Bevaux makes the best cantonment that we have struck this far. The only objection is that the buildings make a grand target for the Boche in case they decide to start something. So far, it has been pleasantly quiet. On our occasional trips back-country we see evidences of considerable activity, but this seems to be concentrated on our left. We have heard that the Germans have made a more or less successful attack in the British sector to the north in April. What the details are we do not know, but there is every indication that it was so successful, that the whole Allied line is on pins and needles awaiting the next move that is sure to follow. Hell is bound to break out somewhere and not too far in the distant future, as the Germans are certainly not going to pass up the chance of making one last attempt to break through before the Americans can be pushed forward in any great numbers. Whatever their plans may be, I am sure that they do not contemplate anything serious in this sector, or probably they are fooling us. A *coup de main* the other night was successful in that they brought back a German officer. The very best "Third Degree" methods of the French could not squeeze any information from the poor fellow. I doubt that he knew any more than we do, but he had to undergo the ordeal just the same.

Verdun – April 27th

My dear Mother,

I haven't written since the letters in which I told you all about my trip to Aix-les-Bains. I think that I mentioned in one of my letters that upon my arrival back to the section, I found that we had moved again to the front. I think that I also mentioned that we had a new lieutenant, a much older man named Seward.

We are cantoned this time in rather comfortable quarters, our headquarters being in an old Army barracks just across the river from the Citadel of Verdun. The barracks are called Caserne Bevaux, and are located in the *faubourgs* (suburbs) called Pavé and Belleville. Our runs take us to the most northerly part of the Verdun sector, our division, the 20th D.I., occupying the famous old battlegrounds of the 1916 Verdun attack. They are holding what is left of the old forts, Douamont and Vaux, and also the shattered remains of the villages of Fleury and Bras.

One of our posts is at an old quarry called the Carrière d'Houdemont. Another post is at Bras, and then we have cars on call at posts called Nice and Berges. All of these posts are, of course, merely dugouts, and they are so located that we find it very dangerous in making the trips back and forth. The trip up to Houdemont is particularly dangerous, the road traversing for some distance a small valley called Vale du Mort. It was here that in

Postcard of Main St. in Bras.

1916 so many thousands of both French and Germans were slaughtered. One of the French doctors told me that over 50,000 men lay buried at this spot. So many, in fact, that if they were to be suddenly called back to life, they would be so crowded that they would not be able to stand up. Arms and legs and other body fragments lie exposed in all directions, the result of almost constant bombardment, and the smell of the place is not at all to our liking. There is a place near Fleury that is pointed out to us as the place where a whole platoon were buried alive as they stood in the trenches on alert, the result of an exploding mine; the tops of their bayonets are still visible.

We are all hoping that the sector remains quiet while we are up here, as it sure would be hell if anything important were to happen that would require our making trips under such terrific difficulties. It's bad enough now, as we are compelled to watch for shells coming from all directions, as we are at the peak of a salient which is surrounded by the Boche on three sides. Our every movement is spotted by the German observation balloons, as there is not a tree left standing in all this region, and I am told that the country was sufficiently wooded before the fun began.

The Battlefield.

Verdun – May 1st

My Dear Mother,

We are still up here, doing little but marking time and waiting for something to happen. The weather is getting warmer, and it is so good to lie out in the open and absorb a little sunlight. The roads are drying up and driving is becoming easier every day. Things are unusually quiet, so quiet in fact, that one becomes reckless and takes chances that you would never think of taking. Dandelions have begun to appear and the fellows, especially the French, scurry around for them, exposing themselves quite dangerously. We don't get much green stuff over here, and that is why the men take such chances in getting the dandelions in order to make salads.

I had a bad scare the other day. I had just returned from a run and was parking my car at the post at Houdemont. The *brancardiers* were all out, sitting and standing around the entrance of the *abri*, enjoying the afternoon sun. I finished backing up my car and was at the rear, letting down the tail board, when I heard a shell come ripping in. Force of habit made me drop to the ground as the damn thing hit, right in the little courtyard in front of the *abri*. The shell had landed so near that the concussion fairly stunned me. I soon recovered my senses in time to crawl under the car and avoid the shower of rocks and debris that descended.

Looking out from under, I saw a lousy sight: six men lay in front of the *abri* door. I don't have to go into details, but the place was a mess. I stayed where I was to be reasonably sure that another shell was not coming along and then crawled out. Two men had come up from the *abri* by this time, and with their help we picked up the pieces. Three were absolutely done for, but the other three seemed to have some life left. We went over them carefully to find all the holes, and then when they were sufficiently bandaged to carry, loaded them into the car and went like hell for the triage. Although my car was pierced by numerous shell fragments, the engine and tires were intact. When I arrived at the triage, I found that one had died on the way in. There were 16 holes in one of the boys who lived; he was more like a sieve than a man.

If that shell had come in a minute later, I would have taken it with the rest of them. Is it any wonder that we over here develop a peculiar philosophy that is decidedly fatalistic. I like to feel that one of those shells has my number on it, and until it is fired I will get along all right. So, there is nothing to do but sit tight and wait for the end, if there ever will be such a thing.

Life moves along about as usual, although the new lieutenant has tightened up on discipline and has tried in many ways to make us realize that we are a regular army unit at last. This comes rather hard as we have been working for such a long time under the slip-shod, but efficient discipline that is common in the French army. The French officers have become, let us say, mellowed by their long experience in the war, and are therefore quite content to let well enough alone. Not that there is a lack of discipline in the French army, but they have learned to overlook or refuse to enforce the many little annoying regulations which make military life so aggravating to the average private. The result is that the men are in the main contented and willing to always do their share of the work.

I am afraid that I have already incurred the animosity of our new lieutenant. I have had several run-ins with him already, all coming from his inability to understand the old methods of doing things up here. I was told one day to make a trip with an officer to the H.O.E. at Glorieux. The order came from the Medicine chef and I made the trip, in spite of the fact that I was aware of the new order from the American lieutenant that we should not take these extra trips unless we had received permission from him. As the trip was urgent, I failed to get his permission, and so when he heard that I had made the trip he was furious and had me on the carpet.

Emerging from an abri.

I had nothing to say but reported the incident to the Medicine Chef on my next trip out. He in turn was furious and immediately got in touch with Seward and had him on the carpet. Nobody gets quite so mad as a Frenchman when he feels that his authority has been questioned. He let it be known that if the section was to continue serving with the 20th D.I., all orders given by the French personnel should have preference over any orders or regulations that the American lieutenant might announce. This bawling out make Seward all the more sore at me, so I find that I am what the boys call "S.O.L."

This antagonism between the lieutenant and myself makes me all the more discontented with this life. After all, I have seen all there is to be seen in this particular work and I would like to take a shot at something else. Several of the old fellows have made applications for a change of service, and I think that I will do likewise. Kirk Meadowcroft got a transfer to the Intelligence Department the other day, and I told him to see if he could not work out something for me. I would like to take a shot at aviation. The few times that I have been up have been great, and you would sure get your run for the money up there. How would you like the idea if I decided to make the change?

Verdun – May 16th

My Dear Mother,

Still here with nothing much of importance to tell you about. Things continue to be very quiet, although there is a decided feeling of unrest and expectancy prevailing. We all wonder what is going to happen and where. Certainly one or the other of the opposing forces will take advantage of this stretch of splendid weather that we have been enjoying for the last month. It isn't right that everything should be so quiet.

More detailed information has begun to sift in concerning the activities in the British front during the last days of March and the first of April. It appears that the Germans were quite successful and managed to make a very decided dent in the lines east of Montdidier. Certainly hope that they concentrate their activity on our left, as I have little desire to be mixed up in anything at the present time.

You will probably remember that I was vaccinated before leaving the states. Well, that operation acted as did the numerous others that I had taken; it did not take. I thought that I was immune to that antitoxin, but I am mistaken. I was re-vaccinated the other day by one of the French doctors, and believe me, that took. They vaccinated me three times at once, and the result is that my arm is as big as the moon and very, very sore. That is one of the reasons that I have not written of late. The other is that one of the cuts on my hand has become infected and it is almost impossible for me to hold a pen or pencil. But both annoyances are clearing up quickly and I feel that I will be alright in a short time.

It is always very interesting to read the reports of your activities back home. One would think that it would be impossible to raise all the money that is being subscribed to the Liberty Loan Drives. And it sure is funny to hear about all your heatless and meatless days and the laws about the use of sugar. But we over here often wonder where all these vast supplies that you are saving go to. We certainly haven't seen anything of them over here. Sugar is just as scarce as it ever was, and when we get some white flour, it is a cue for rejoicing. American cigarettes are still scarce, although the Red Cross does sometimes come through with a few cartons. The Y.M.C.A. charges exorbitant prices for the chocolate and cigarettes that they have, with the result that we can't afford to buy them. This makes us sore as we understand that the cigarettes and things have been donated to the Y.M.C.A., and we can't understand why they must charge us for everything.

"Things continue to be very quiet."

Part 5

Late Spring and Summer of 1918

The Ludendorff Offensive

Introduction

In the spring and early summer of 1918 the German high command decided to launch one last, desperate offensive to end the war on favorable terms. Eric Ludendorff gathered the pick of his combat troops for a series of lightning-fast strikes at Allied lines in the center of the Western Front. These produced immediate and dramatic gains in territory and in captured prisoners.

By skillful manipulation of reserves and diversion of battle units, the French and British were able to blunt the assaults, which over a period of two months simply ran out of momentum, out of supplies and out of fresh manpower. The Allies were then quick to mount effective counterattacks that presaged the final, victorious Allied drive to the Rhine River, culminating in the general armistice of November 11th, 1918. It was during this action that Wolfe earned the Croix de Guerre.

Wolfe's account of the Battle of Bois Belleau, or Belleau Wood, the first significant victory for the Americans, and in particular the US Marines, questions the popular interpretation of this engagement.

Ligny-en-Barrois – May 1st

Out again and I don't know where to this time. The division received orders to pull out on the 19th, and we left our comfortable quarters at the Barracks of Bevaux on the 20th. Down through the familiar country on the way to Bar-le-Duc, and then, to our surprise, we pull up at good old Ligny. How different it looks now in the summertime, with all the trees in leaf and flowers in profusion everywhere you look. It sure was cold when we pulled in here the last time, not five months ago. I don't think I ever felt the cold so much as that first night that I spent sleeping in my car. But that all seems very far away now. We have good quarters in a nice clean barn in the outskirts of the town, and we are looking forward to a nice long *repos* under these pleasant conditions.

As the cars are all in good shape, we will have practically nothing to do but enjoy ourselves. Have already been up to the old Hotel Cheval Blanc to renew acquaintances, and expect to make a trip to Bar as soon as we receive permission.

Mealtime.

Homer Gage, one of the old section fellows, is going on permission tomorrow. He is taking his dog Gipsy with him with the hope that in some way he will be able to send the dog home to his parents. He has become very much attached to the dog, a Belgian Police dog, and when the order came through the other day that no livestock was to be carried with the section, Homer decided that he could not give the dog away and that he would try to send it home. The other dogs in the section were given to French friends before we left Verdun, and so now we have no more pets.

We passed lots of troops on the way down from Verdun. They were all traveling to the west. Looks as if the powers that be anticipated something. But sure hope that nothing happens to interfere with our long looked for *repos*. Ran into some Americans this morning who are quartered down the road towards the Vosges. They had just come over and had lots of interesting things to tell us about the activities back home. According to their story, there are a great many more American troops in France that any one of us had surmised. This certainly made us all feel good as we all feel sure that they will be sorely needed in the near future. Will write now more often as we will have little to do, and I always feel more like writing when we are *en repos*.

May 28th – Ligny-en-Barrois

Dear Mother,

This will be a very hurried letter, as we are in the midst of great excitement. Apparently, the Germans have at last started their long awaited push. And according to all reports, it seems to be going places with a vengeance.

We were all out working on our cars this morning when we first heard of the exciting events. The Lieutenant had been called to the G.B.D. headquarters earlier that morning, and about 11:00 he came tearing back in the staff car, and finding the majority of us at the cars, lost no time in giving his orders.

We were to prepare to get under way at once. Our division, the 20th. D.I., was already en route and we were to lose no time in following along. That was all that we could learn at that time, but later in the afternoon, while we were waiting for the *camion* to get loaded, Woolley told us what the Lieutenant had passed on to him.

The Germans had broken through the lines at a point in the Chemin des Dames west of Rheims, and were pushing along at a great rate towards the Marne, at Château-Thierry. The whole Allied line seemed to have been caught off guard, and as a result, things are very much in the state of chaos. It is hoped that our division will in some way help to stem the tide, but our orders are to keep in touch with the division at all times and to retreat with them, in case they are compelled to fall back. This sort of sounds as if they expect us to be on the go for the next few days.

You can well imagine how excited we all are, as this will be the first time that we have had the opportunity to engage in what promises to be a thrilling retreat. Word just came through that Section Thirty, serving in the Chemin des Dames, has lost five cars and that two of their men have been captured.

Well, I don't know as to whether or not I would like to be captured, but it will be a change from the terrible monotony of our old front line work to have the possibility of capture in the back of one's mind. I am giving this letter to a French civilian friend of mind who promises to address the envelope and post it to you. In this way I will be able to get around the censors.

May 27th – June 1st, 1918

What follows is a resume of notes and pages from a diary written in lieu of letters that it was impossible to write during this period.

Orders came on the morning of May 28th. We were to follow our old division, the 20th D.I., into action. Conditions indicated that something very important was afoot. We were to be under way by three in the afternoon, at the latest. As word of our move had arrived during the late morning, we hardly had sufficient time to load our cars and the *camions*. The atmosphere was charged with expectation and we were all terribly inquisitive as to the reason for our unexpected move. Orders called for our making a contact with the divisional G.B.D. in the vicinity of Dormans. More than that nobody knew. It wasn't until the next morning that we learned what had happened and what we were expected to do.

*German advance May 17–June 3, 1918. Daily chart of front lines in formation of
Château Thierry Salient.*

The Germans had at last broken through, vindicating our latent fear that they
would strike before the Americans could be concentrated in any great numbers to oppose
their advance. The reports that we finally received were vague and in many instances,
conflicting. But the fact remained that an attack of terrific intensity had been launched the
morning of the 27th of May, in what is commonly called the Chemin des Dames sector,

all along that front from Berry-au-Bac on the east to Pontoise on the west. Apparently, the move was in no way expected by the Allies, who were completely surprised by the suddenness and intensity of the onslaught.

The Chemin des Dames sector had been completely inactive since General Neville's abortive attempts in 1917. It was considered a rest sector. Here, divisions that had been through an intensive period of fighting were sent to recuperate and recruit their depleted forces to fighting strength. At the time of the attack, several units of the British Army, the Ninth Corps of the 6th Army, which had received such a terrific beating earlier in the spring around Lys, and five divisions of French, comprised the bulk of the defense. They formed their own reserves, as the main body of reserves had been concentrated behind the lines to the west of Soissons and back of the British sector, where the attack had been anticipated. Some 47 divisions of the very flower of the German Army, the equivalent of 60 divisions of French, had been concentrated in the narrow strip of territory between Laon and Neufchâtel. This force was supported by 1,450 batteries of artillery, the greatest known concentration of artillery since the beginning of the war.

Why the Allies were unable to get information about this tremendous concentration is hard to understand. They were caught absolutely flatfooted. And before they could rally assistance to the woefully weak and absolutely inadequate defense, the Boche had carried well on to completion what promised for a time to be the greatest catastrophe of the war.

Their initial thrust had proven so successful that they immediately widened their front to the west, taking Fort Malmaison in stride and reaching the southern bank of the Aisne before noon of the 27th. Here a brief halt to consolidate their positions and then word came to carry on to the south. They met practically no resistance during the afternoon as the English were now in full retreat, and the small numbers of French fell slowly back to the heights of Rheims. Near Laffaux, the members of the French 21st Regiment fought to the last man in their effort to stem the advance. Great numbers of Allied prisoners were taken, and their forward thrusts came so quickly that quantities of ammunition and supplies of all sorts were captured before the Allies had time to destroy them. By evening of the 27th they had reached the Vesle, an advance of twelve miles since morning, and, having crossed the river at numerous points, occupied the towns of Fismes, Vasseny and Bazoches. Quite a remarkable advance. And all accomplished in one short day. So much for the 27th of May.

The 28th dawned hot and clear. During that night a momentous conclave of the German leaders at the Spa could hardly believe the reports of their success. At last they could satisfy the victory-hungry masses behind the lines who had been demanding, more and more vehemently, a tangible offering to appease their many years of poverty and suffering. Papers throughout Germany herald the action as the beginning of the end—the long-prayed-for victory for German arms. The prime objective of the operation was to penetrate sufficiently to the east of Soissons so as to threaten an encircling movement of this key position. In this way they hoped to draw off the Allied reserves from the British front. Turning quickly from the Chemin des Dames, the plan was then to strike with terrific force at the weakened British lines, and force passage through to the English Channel. Having in this manner severed the Allied lines of defense, they had every reason to believe that the complete collapse of the Allied defense would swiftly follow. The British would be trapped in the narrow confines of western Belgium, and the French and Americans would soon give

Ruin of shelled church.

up the futile defense of Paris. If Paris could be taken, the war would be over.

This deceptive thrust had proven successful beyond all comprehension. In spite of their unfortunate experience of four years before, the Germans decided to forgo momentarily their drive to the Channel, and follow up their success of the day before by penetrating farther to the south, hoping in this way to cross the Marne, cut the Paris to Châlons railroad and sever the Allied armies of the west and east. But they must broaden the head of the salient or otherwise run the danger of thrusting their head into an encircling flank movement. So the next morning, May the 28th, the drive to the south was continued while strong forces were sent against the eastern and western flanks. As on the 27th, the advance proved unbelievably easy, the futile efforts of a few scattered units offering the only resistance. At dusk of the 28th they had crossed the Vesle and penetrated as far south as Courville, having taken the villages of Fismes, Cuiry-Housse and Chéry. On the east, they took Thil and pushed to the outskirts of Courcy and the fort at Brimont. On the west, they were equally successful, reaching the outskirts of Soissons, taking Missy and Venizel.

It was to face this striding monster, flush with easy victory, that our little division, the 20th D.I., was so hurriedly aroused from its well deserved rest at Ligny, and sent blindly into the breech. Driving steadily through that afternoon and evening, the section made good time until we passed Châlons and headed for Epernay. The road now became almost impassable. *Camions* filled with sleepy men were trying to make their way through the never-ending line of civilians, on foot and in every sort of contrivance, all heading southward, fleeing the vengeance of the approaching Boche. As dawn began to break, it was decided to cut to the south and then approach Dormans from Montmort. We made better time for a while and then again had to fairly force our way through the endless lines of carts and carriages of every description. It was a pathetic sight. Here were hundreds of families literally torn up by the roots. With no place to go, they trudged southward, wearily carrying on their backs the few things of value that they were able to get together before they were driven from their homes.

To add to the general congestion, we came upon great numbers of British troops straggling along to the south, their guns and heavy equipment having been thrown away, and some even mounted on artillery horses. Their only reply to our hails was, "I say. What is the shortest way to Paris?" I admit receiving a very poor impression of the intestinal fortitude of the British Tommy. It was my first glimpse of a defeated, retreating army, and I was undoubtedly prejudiced.

When it became apparent that our progress as a convoy was to be greatly retarded, our French lieutenant pushed on ahead, hoping to make a contact with the G.B.D. and thereby save a lot of valuable time. We had just passed Condé-en-Brie when he overtook us. We were to establish a temporary base at some bridgehead on the southern bank of the Marne, pick up a *brancardier* and then push to the north, taking care of what wounded we might come across. As no attempt had been made to establish dressing stations or a Triage, we were to take our cases to Montmirail, some forty kilometers away to the south, the only hospital accessible to the region.

With these meager instructions, the section headed for the bridgehead at Jaulgonne. We arrived at the town of Varennes, on the southern bank of the river, opposite Jaulgonne, at about eleven in the morning. A large field to the south of the town was picked out as the Parc, and we hurriedly unloaded our cars. Six of the cars were sent to the north over the Jaulgonne bridge, while six more were sent to the west, planning to cross at Dormans and proceed towards Ville-en-Tardenois. I was part of the Dormans detachment, and had as my

Washing our clothes.

passenger the Medicine Major of the Division. When we were well on our way, I ventured to ask the Major where we could expect to contact the Division. He frankly admitted that he had no idea. The first contingents had arrived early in the morning of May 29th. They had hastily made arrangements to dig in, but before they could secure a foot-hold, the Boche were upon them in such overwhelming numbers that they began a slow retreat. They were making a stubborn resistance before Ville-en- Tardenois, and it was towards this town that we were heading.

Having no idea as to what was happening in front of us, we went along very slowly, not knowing at what turn of the road we might run into the advancing Boche. The Major told me that the Boche had captured four men and eight cars of Section Thirty the day before. You may be sure that we had little desire to run into the same fate.

We finally came into sight of Ville-en-Tardenois. The firing ahead of us was quite *brisque*. We were thankful, however, that neither side had had opportunity to bring up their artillery, so the firing was all machine gun and rifle. We shot into town, glad to reach the protection of the buildings. We stopped at a house flying a red cross. A dressing station had been established here and the place was already full of cases.

Five of the cars were loaded and sent to the south, with directions to stop at Varennes and send up replacements. Although there were two slight cases remaining, the Major refused to let me go, saying that he wished to stay a while. I had the greatest desire to be on my way back as the fighting now seemed to be carried right into the town, to the north. It was getting too close for comfort. I went out and started the car, hoping in this way to suggest leaving to the Major, but nothing doing. Some soldiers came running down the street towards us. They dispersed into the houses and emerged with furniture and other things with which they built a crude barricade behind which they mounted a light machine gun. Just about the same time, a *brancardier*, who had been watching things from the rear of the house, announced that the Boche were plainly visible coming over the top of the hill to our left. We ran back; sure enough, there they were.

At last the Major seemed to have had sufficient notice. He jumped into the front seat with me and, with the *brancardiers* hanging on as best they could, we beat a hasty retreat. I was never so happy to leave a place in all my life. The old bus fairly flew, and we didn't stop until we had reached Verneuil. Here I dropped the Major and headed for Varennes.

Making my report at Varennes, I started on the long trip to Montmirail. Traffic was heavy and I had some difficulty finding the hospital. It took me over four hours to complete the trip of eighty kilometers. I found that the section had moved its *parc* to Celles-lès-Condé during my absence. I had hoped to get a rest, but after getting a load of *essence*, I was ordered to Courmont.

On the way up, I witnessed one of the most exciting events in all my experience. About two kilometers this side of Courmont, our way was obstructed by a group of *camions* who were unloading a battalion of soldiers. It was well along in the evening, almost dark in fact. Suddenly, out of the north, just skimming the tree tops, two German planes roared on us. At almost point-blank range, their machine guns fairly riddled the men who lined both sides of the road. Stunned by the suddenness of the attack, the men could do little but fall to the ground. Still in a fog, they picked themselves up, only to find that the Boche had zoomed around and were coming back at us. I was under my car by this time and as many of the soldiers as were able had scrambled under the *camions*. The planes swept down at us again with their guns going full force, banked sharply after passing, and disappeared into the northern twilight.

It was a perfect job of air-strafing. Nearly half of the battalion were either killed or wounded. What were left soon started up the road and disappeared over the hill. With what meager supplies we had on hand, we made the wounded as comfortable as possible. I

French anti-aircraft gun in action.

had some difficulty in persuading the *camion* officers to carry the wounded back as far as Dormans, but they finally consented. So the trucks that only a short time before unloaded their human cargo, were engaged in taking what was left of some fifty of them back to the hospital. A very quick turnover.

I led the *camions* back to the G.B.D. at Dormans. Here the wounded were unloaded and I continued on my way to Montmirail, stopping en route at the section *parc*, to report the emergency at Dormans. How I made that trip I don't know. I must have fallen asleep several times as I drove the long forty miles. Not since the night of the 27th had I been able to get any sleep. I finally reached the hospital at Montmirail, unloaded, and started on the long trek back. But I soon found that it was impossible to go on. So, utterly exhausted, I drove the car into a field beside the road, climbed into the rear of the car and was immediately asleep.

The Germans that day, May 29th, had continued their advance to the south as far as Gourmont, taking Fère-en-Tardenois in the afternoon. In the west, their drive at Soissons

French machine-gun on Champagne Front.

was stubbornly resisted by the 48th French Colonial D.I., which had hurriedly been brought up to support the demoralized 6th Army. Their attempts to the east had met with little success, the famous defenses of Rheims remaining impregnable. Convinced by this time that this general attack was no mere feint, the Allies moved quickly to prevent further losses.

Conceding the Germans' ability to reach the Marne, they planned to stop them at that point by massing great numbers of artillery units along the heights on the southern bank. Their finest fighting divisions were sent to the left and right with instructions to prevent, at any cost, the widening of the mouth of the salient. So, what was left of our little division, the 20th D.I., was allotted the thankless task of retarding, as much as possible, the main drive at the center. That they succeeded in preventing the Germans' arrival at the Marne until the 30th of May is an everlasting tribute to their unbelievable tenacity. By the evening of May 30th, the Allies had prepared a defense of the Marne that was to prove impregnable.

May the 30th. I awoke just as dawn was breaking, stiff, tired, cold and hungry. Cranking up, I was on my way, arriving at Celles-lès-Condé at about seven. I spotted François in the kitchen trailer and so was able to get a cup of coffee and a snack to eat. All the cars were out except two that were being worked on by the mechanics. I took my time in filling up with *essence* and oil, hoping that I would be allowed to get some more sleep. But nothing doing. Seward spotted me as he drove up in the staff car and ordered me up to Jaulgonne.

Five cars were waiting here on reserve and it looked as if I would be able to get some rest. Not so. My friend, the Medicine Major, drove up in one of the cars coming down from Dormans. He was going up to Le Charmel and, spying me, indicated that I was elected. I liked the old boy, but didn't much relish the trip before me, knowing as I did his propensity to linger in situations that I considered unhealthy. We had all been warned that morning that the bridges had already been mined in anticipation of the Germans reaching the river, and that we should time our return trips so as not to be caught on the other side of the river.

With this thought firmly fixed in my mind, we climbed out of the valley and soon were in Le Charmel. Passing through the barricade at the far side of the town , we continued on the road towards Fère-en-Tardenois. The firing to our front and on our right was increasingly heavy as we slowly made our way to the north. We soon ran into a detachment who stopped us and warned us back, informing us that the Germans were right over the next rise in the road, and advising us that they were falling back on Le Charmel to make their last stand before crossing the river.

So back we went to Le Charmel. I parked my car at the southern outskirts of the town and, leaving it there, walked up to the barricade with the Major. More troops came straggling in and took up positions in the buildings at the north of the town. It seemed silly that these men should risk their lives in attempting to defend a position which was doomed from the very start. Why couldn't they fall back to the river immediately and thereby avoid this needless risk? I made bold to tell the Major of my thoughts. His only reply was a shrug of his shoulders and a *"Cest le guerre."*

We hadn't long to wait, probably a half an hour. It was hot. The sun was directly overhead. To relieve the nervous tension, I walked back and cranked up the old car. I knew that the Major would wait until the last minute, so I wanted to make sure that nothing would hinder our hurried exit. As I rejoined the Major, a burst of machine gun fire at our right announced that the Boche were upon us. I started back to the car and the Major, after one last look from between the houses, ran down the road after me. It was the first time that I had seen the old boy hurry. He was hardly in his seat before I had the old bus in high and was tearing down the road towards Jaulgonne. We hadn't allowed any too much time, for as we passed the last house, we spotted a wave of grey emerging from the woods at our left. They sped us along with a parting fusillade of bullets, three of them going through the rear of the car. Apparently, they cared little for a red cross. But I couldn't really blame them. After all, I was in reality acting as a taxi for an officer, and that wasn't exactly cricket.

We shot down the hill into Jaulgonne. Here we were stopped by a *brancardier* who informed me that there was a load of wounded down the road towards Dormans. So away we went, the Major still with me. We did not have to go far. The cases were loaded and I was on my way back in no time at all. We had almost reached the town when the Major uttered a sharp cry and pointed to the hill tops at our right. There was no mistaking the grey uniforms. A battery of French guns from across the river commenced firing, the shells bursting along the crest of the hill.

Could I make the bridge at Jaulgonne before they blew it up? I took the corner on two wheels and shot down the incline towards the bridge approach. The bridge was still intact. A group of soldiers at the far end of the bridge were frantically waving us back. Evidently the mine fuses had been lighted and we were being warned not to try to cross. I had to think fast. I realized that it would probably be impossible for me to stop the car, and anyway, anything would be better than capture. There was only one thing to do. I gave the old bus everything she had. We hit the approach, bounded into the air, and shot across like a scared jack rabbit over the hump in the middle and down the grade to the far end. A loud report sounded in back of us. The cables had gone, but we had made it. Somehow I managed to pull the car to a stop. I was trembling like a leaf, scared to death. I looked at the Major. His face was white as a sheet. I have no doubt but that mine was in the same condition. He gave me a sickly smile, patted me on the back and got out of the car without saying a word.

A group of engineers came running up to offer their congratulations. I left the Major to do the talking and started my long trip to Montmirail. Driving into Celles-lès-Condé, I was stopped by Bingham, who told me that the section had again moved , this time to Baulne-en-Brie on the road to Montmort. I told him that the bridge was down at Jaulgonne, and asked if all the cars had been heard from. He didn't know. But he informed me that the bridge at Dormans was down and that Chateau was the only bridgehead that hadn't been destroyed.

I made good time to Montmirail, unloaded my car and asked if there was any place where I might get something to eat. I was told that there was an American Red Cross hut in town. I had some difficulty in finding it, but it proved well worth my while. They proved to be a great bunch, four women and two men. Put me up to a grand feed and even came across with chocolate and cigarettes. They told me that they had received orders to be prepared to pull out at any moment. They indicated that the morale behind the lines was at a pretty low ebb. The influx of refugees had made it necessary for them to be on the job every minute. A pretty tired and discouraged bunch, but doing a great job too. My opinion that the Boche would undoubtedly be checked at the Marne seemed to cheer them up immeasurably. It was not until 8:00 that I reluctantly left and headed for the river.

May 30th marked the height of the German success. Although they made some notable advances the following day, their comparatively easy advances of from ten to fifteen kilometers a day, along a fifty mile front, had come to an end. The French colonial divisions, ably supported by the French regulars and later by the astonishing Americans, had again proven their ability to rise to unbelievable heights of bravery in the face of overwhelming odds. During the next few days, division after division of the very finest German troops were to be thrown at these fierce defenders, only to be beaten back with terrific losses. The tide had definitely turned. Once again the Kaiser had to find his troops within striking distance of that tantalizing objective, Paris, only to be turned back at its very doors.

Continuing their advance in the middle of the salient on the morning of the 30th,

French field hospital on Champagne Front.

the Germans met with only scattered and feeble resistance. One thrust reached the Marne at Jaulgonne about 6:00 in the afternoon. Another reached the river shortly before, at Brasles. Dashing to the west, this contingent reached the outskirts of Château-Thierry. Here they found the going decidedly difficult. The vicious 33rd Colonials virtually decimated their every attempt to enter the town and reach the bridge.

On the right they had reached Dormans and Vincelles, but at no place had they been able to cross the Marne. The western tip of the salient had been thrown back slightly but only at terrific losses. Soissons had fallen during the early morning attacks, but the Foreign Legion, taking up their stand on the Montagne de Paris near Ambleny, had refused to be budged. To their right, the Zouaves and Algerian Tirailleurs fought off their continued waves of attack so stubbornly that it was not until late afternoon that the villages of Hartennes and Oulchy finally fell into their hands. At the extreme west, the 170th D.I., resisting valiantly, was forced back north of the Aisne, bringing the line back to Pontoise.

The eastern tip of the salient, the defenses of Rheims, again remained impregnable, but only due to the stubborn efforts of the 45th D.I. Further to the south, the Germans enjoyed better fortunes. Ville-en-Tardenois was occupied early in the afternoon and the

French were compelled to fall back on the Heights of Rheims. The Germans had every reason to be satisfied with their efforts for the day. But their casualties had been enormous. Practically seventy-five percent of their forces had been thrown into the assault and they still were a long way from Paris.

On my trip back to the Marne that late evening, I passed one of the motorized battalions of the American Army, on their way up. It turned out to be the battalion of the 3rd American Division, which took such a prominent part in the defense of Château-Thierry the next day. It seems to have become rather legendary to think of the defense of Château-Thierry in terms of the Marines. But it was this unit of the 3rd Division, and a few days later, the 23rd and 9th regulars of the 2nd Division, who were first on the scene and carried the brunt of these attacks. The Marines seem to have received all the credit.

I arrived back at Baulne at about eleven in the evening, serviced my car and reported at the section H.Q., expecting to be sent forward once more. But the lieutenant surprised me by saying that he did not think I would be needed until the next morning. Having reached the Marne, the Boche seemed to be content to wait until morning before attempting to cross. As the road along the river lay in full view of the Germans on the other side, the section had been ordered not to make any but the most urgent trips in the daytime.

This unexpected opportunity to get surely needed sleep, the night of May 31st, was put to good advantage. I searched through several deserted houses until I found one that met my fancy and proceeded to make myself at home. My room for the evening was the boudoir of some demoiselle, who evidently had left in a hurry, leaving drawers full of flimsy underthings and other evidences of feminine occupancy. The bed was neatly made and the bed clothes were even turned down. Apparently, the alarm had come just as my unknown hostess was preparing for bed.

Feeling the pangs of hunger, I took my searchlight and went downstairs. The kitchen was well- stocked with preserves and, better still, I found the carcass of a partially consumed chicken in what served as a cold closet. Everything remained just as they had been compelled to leave it a few hours before. You might think that the owners had just stepped out and would be back in a short time.

I felt decidedly as if I were an intruder, but I must admit that I had no compunction in enjoying whatever comforts the house afforded. After all, the Boche might well be in this very house in a few hours. If not desecrated by the Huns, the place would surely be torn apart by the Allied troops who would pillage the district on the morrow. I had seen it happen only too many times the last few days. Allied troops invariably pillage the homes of the French civilians through which they pass while retreating. I suppose that this action is condoned by the theory that nothing of value should be left behind for the enemy, and perhaps that is as it should be. After all, it can be expected that the Germans will leave nothing intact, in the event that the fortunes of war compel them to vacate occupied territory. So why look askance at the pillaging of the French soldiers themselves.

But it certainly is difficult to comprehend the extent of the depredations committed by the Allied troops in the houses of their own compatriots. And in the cases where the German advances never penetrate to the full extent of the French evacuation, the results are not at all pleasing. Hundreds of refugees returned to their firesides to find them lying in an incredible mess, full of needless filth, contents of bureaus and chests dumped recklessly on the floor, dishes, pictures, mirrors and furniture ruthlessly smashed to bits, mattresses disemboweled, odds and ends of clothing and linen strewn on the floor, heedlessly trampled on by the feet of their own brave defenders. To return to such apparently unwarranted devastation of practically all they possessed must have left the unfortunate civilians pondering the futility of man's very existence.

The sun was well up in the heavens when I was awakened the next morning, May 31st, by a thunderous explosion, seemingly in my room. Stupid from sleeping so heavily, I managed to extricate myself from the enfolding comfort of the French mattress and staggered to the window. The peaceful little town was undergoing its baptism of fire. Evidently, the Germans had managed to bring up their field pieces during the night. The arrival of another shell uncomfortably near made me scurry for my clothes and beat a hasty retreat for the cellar, a much safer place to finish my toilet. The shelling soon stopped and my stomach suggesting, I made my way to the kitchen trailer, parked in the outskirts of the town. Shorty Mills joined me in a cup of coffee, and from him I learned the events of the evening.

The Germans had not crossed the river that night, May the 30th, but they had reached the Marne River at all points from beyond Dormans on the east to Château-Thierry on the west. Our division was scattered along the southern bank of the river, using the railroad embankment as their main defense. Shorty had made a couple of trips that night around the Verennes bend to Sauvigny, and he reported that the going was decidedly dangerous. The Boche were shelling the road with their field pieces, and in addition, were raking it every so often with machine gun fire. We were allowed to go only as far as Crézancy in the daytime and even at that point it was decidedly unhealthy. Shorty went off to get some needed sleep, and I decided to shave off a few days growth of beard.

Getting some hot water from the chef, I started lathering my face. I had just about finished this process when some more shells came pounding in. Leaving my shaving kit on the side of the car, I dove into the nearest cellar and waited for the storm to blow over. When I came up, I was surprised to find that someone had made off with my razor, a nice straight edge that I had prized for many years. I was about to wipe off the lather and give up the thought of shaving when I happened to remember that someone had sent me a safety razor in one of my Xmas boxes. I found it after a good deal of looking and managed to complete the job. It was the first time that I had used a safety razor and so I had quite a time mastering its peculiarities.

That morning, May 31st, was in every way perfect. A bright sun shone overhead and the air was warm and clear. I fiddled around my car a bit and finally wandered up to the house which the Lieutenant had taken over for his quarters. Woolley and Wholey were in the staff car parked in front, and, in answer to my queries, they replied that there was little activity and that the Lieutenant was up at D.I. headquarters in conference with the Medicine Chef. It had been very quiet during the night and most of the men were scattered around the town knocking off some sleep. Doug volunteered that the Third American Division was expected to relieve us. As soon as this was accomplished, we would pull out of this vicinity

Gordon Rogers shaving.

with our division. The 20th D.I. had been pretty badly decimated in this last party. Over half of the men had been either captured or wounded, and the ones who were left certainly had earned a rest. We all hoped that they would not be compelled to bear the brunt of the attacks that the Germans were bound to make in attempting to cross the Marne.

Our gab-fest was interrupted by the arrival of a man on a bicycle from one of the artillery outfits. One of the guns had blown up and there was a carload of wounded to carry back. I was elected, and putting the wheel in the back of the car, I shot away with the messenger as my guide. I was directed back towards Condé and then up the hill at the right over a bad road, into the woods that covered the top of the hills to the north. Here we found the battery in position, and while the car was being loaded, I walked towards the crest of the hill where an officer was peering through glasses at the hills on the other side of the river. He let me take his glasses. The panorama that stretched out before me was very interesting. Varennes lay at the foot of the hill and Jaulgonne was plainly visible just across the river. Back of Jaulgonne, the road to Fère wound its way up the ravine and disappeared into the woods that obscured everything but the roofs of the town of Le Charmel. There seemed to be a good deal of traffic on this road. As I watched, several grey-coated figures came into view from one of the buildings in Jaulgonne and walked casually down towards the river bank. I returned the glasses to the officer. He suggested that the Germans were evidently planning their expected attempt to cross the river that night.

I would have liked to stay there all day but my car was loaded by this time, so I regretfully took leave of the officer and made my way back to the car. I sure had a load, three lying cases and two *assis*. It was a long trip back to Montmirail, but the day was perfect and I realized that there was no cause to hurry. On the way down, I passed more Americans than I thought were in all of France. They were a much better looking bunch than the first Americans I had seen up at Verdun. Like all fresh troops that have never tasted the experiences of war, they all seemed impatient to get to the front and prove their superiority to the despised Boche. They would soon learn better.

After unloading my cases at the R.R. Station, I made my way to the Red Cross shack and again received a hearty welcome. In this hospitable atmosphere, I lingered as long as I thought advisable and then started back. Along the road, I picked up an American officer and gave him a lift as far as Condé. He was attached to the Third American Division. He explained that all the Americans I had seen that day were 3rd Division men. To my amazement, an American division has a full strength organization of about 27,000 men as compared with a French division of about 10,000 men. It was the first time that the 3rd had been in action and he himself had just come over. He had a lot of interesting things to tell me about things in general back in the good old U.S.A.

I was back at the section again about six, just in time to finish off a very much appreciated meal. Most of the fellows were around, and as we were lingering over our *pinard*, the Lieutenant made his appearance and told us that we would probably have a hard night as the Germans would undoubtedly try to get across the river during the night. Six cars were to go to Crèzancy as soon as it was dark and operate from there on call. The other cars were to park at Condé and replace the cars coming down from Crèzancy. We were busy that night. I made three trips before daylight. One I shall never forget.

The Boche started things as soon as it was dark. They threw a nasty barrage on all the roads, and judging from the noise, they probably received as good as they sent, for the woods around us were fairly thick with 75's which were going off incessantly. The cars from Crèzancy soon started to come in and it was my turn to make the trip about 10:00. I reached Crèzancy without any difficulty and was told to proceed to Varennes.

With the exception of having to cross a trench that had been thrown across the road at the north side of the town, the road was clear, but it was taking a terrific beating from the German artillery. There was nothing to do but step on the gas, hope that nothing would hit you and that you would not run into any shell holes. I shot through Moulins, and after crossing the R.R. tracks, I heaved a sigh of relief as I finally gained the comparative shelter of the houses of Varennes. I got out of the car and tried to find someone. Not a person in sight. The place seemed deserted. An extra ferocious blast of machine gun fire to my left, along the railroad bed, made me decide that this was no place to loiter. So I jumped back into the car and turned back to the main road and started in the direction of Courthièzy. I soon ran across a group of divisional *brancardiers* who were wheeling some wounded on one of their stretcher-carriers. I drew up in the protection of some trees and helped them place the wounded in the back of my car. I learned from the *brancardiers* that the Germans had crossed the river on pontoons but were being held at the railroad. Varren's R.R. station was occupied by the Germans, but the division was making a stubborn resistance at this point and it was hoped that they would be able to hold them. I reported this information as I made my way through Crèzancy. The trip back to Montmirail was uneventful and I made good time back to Condé. I made two more trips from Crèzancy to Montmirail that night. I was pretty tired at the end of the last trip. The Germans had crossed the river but had been held at the railroad.

Officers conferring.

As the sun came up that morning of the 1st of June, we all heaved a sigh of relief. At last the Germans had been stopped. Could the wearied men of our division continue to hold them until fresh troops could relieve them? We felt confident, and as the day wore on and more and more Americans poured into the district, our spirits arose and we felt sure that the Boche advance was at an end. Surely, they would never be able to overcome the insurmountable task of crossing the river in force in the face of such concentrated artillery fire and the thousands of fresh, eager Americans who were now lying in wait for them, only too eager to prove their fighting qualities.

As the morning advanced we began to hear news from the rest of the line. The Germans had been held all along the river. At Château-Thierry they had managed to take the northern part of the town, but the island and the southern part of the town were still in the hands of the French colonials and the Americans, a detachment of the 7th M.G. corps, who had so stubbornly defended the south bank all that night. Further to the west, the Boche had made some slight advances around the forest of Villers-Cottêrets, but on the right the line had held and the defense of Rheims remained intact.

The first day of June saw the section rolling steadily all the day. Casualties had piled up at various artillery posts, and it was well on towards sundown before we finally got things cleared up. American machine gun units continued to pour into the sector, and we even were afforded a laugh by the antics of an American M.P. directing traffic at Condé. Word got around that the Americans had promised to drive the Germans back across the river before morning.

The road southward from Crèzancy that night was a perfect shambles. The Germans had brought up some of their heavier pieces and laid shells along that road all night long in the attempt to stop all traffic. They did. The only things that moved over that road that night were our cars. As usual we had to keep going regardless of conditions. But our luck held good. Outside of numerous *éclat* holes in the bodies, the cars were all able to run the next morning.

I had received a lucky assignment that evening, and as a result did not make a trip until almost daylight. An artillery P.C. had been established back of St. Eugene, in a more or less protected gully leading up to the plateau above Varennes. I got little or no sleep as I was parked right on top of a battery of 155's, which were firing pretty steadily all night long. The officers said that they were concentrating their fire on the road that led from the forest of Fère, down the gully through le Charmel and into Jaulgonne.

The 155's look very efficient. Their carriages split in the middle and form a very excellent base. I understand that they pivot on a central base like a machine gun and therefore have a lateral range of over fifty degrees. They are effective well over ten miles and have a projectile which weighs well over sixty pounds. They go off with a terrific roar, and a huge flash emits from the gun's muzzle. I should think that they would be rather hard to camouflage.

My ears hurt me terribly until one of the men gave me a wad of cotton to put into my ears. I was relieved when I finally got a load just as dawn was breaking and started out for Montmirail. I passed Rogers and Nash on the way down and found Hagler at the hospital when I arrived. Doc. told me about the strafing of the Crèzency-Condé road during the night and also that he had heard the Americans had driven the Boche back across the river, and in addition had made several successful coup de mains.

I arrived back at the artillery post at about ten of the morning of June 2nd, only to find that the guns had been ordered further to the west. So, my soft job was at an end and I reported back to the section at Baulne. As four cars had gone *en panne* during the night, suffering from bent wish-bones, I was told to be ready to roll at any time, so I filled up with *essence* and oil and went down the street to the kitchens. François hadn't much to eat but I managed to get enough to suffice and then went foraging to see what I could find in the deserted houses. I didn't have much luck as they had all been pretty thoroughly picked over by this time. I spent about fifteen minutes trying to corner a chicken which had evidently been left behind. I had to give up, the darned thing was too elusive. I'll bet it made a good meal for someone.

Shorty Mills came along as I was returning to the G.H.Q. and confided to me that he had found a cache of wine in one of the houses. With a due amount of caution to see that we were not observed, he led me to a house near the center of the town and down into the darkened, cool cellar.

With the aid of a flashlight, we made our way to a small compartment located under the stairs. No fooling, there, bottle after bottle, lined up just waiting for us, was an excellent assortment of vintage wines. I am afraid that Shorty had already indulged to some extent, for the last part of the journey had been made with much mysterious shushings and warnings to be quiet.

This in no way detracted from the mutual enjoyment of the situation, and you may be sure that the two of us, *bon* companions of many a previous escapade, enjoyed the fortunes of war to the fullest. The wine, I believe, was a dry sauterne, the bottles bore no label but I think were dated in some way. We did not emerge from the cool confines of our retreat until almost six that evening and, hard as it is to believe, were able to muster a very passable appearance when we finally decided that our presence at H.Q. might be expected. Luckily we had not been missed, and after mess that evening, we were told that as the division had been almost wholly relieved by the American Third, there was little likelihood of our having as busy a night as we had had the previous evening. The section was to hold six cars at Condé and I was one of those designated.

The night of June 2nd was fairly quiet. The Germans had evidently given up the idea of advancing to the south and, during the days of June 1st and 2nd, had concentrated their attacks on the line to our left. Their plan was quite evident. The full weight of their force was thrown at the line just south of the Villers-Cottêrets forest, while another frontal attack of great intensity was flung at the line north of Compiègne. Their strategy was to compel the evacuation of the Villers-Cottêrets forest· This meant the fall of Compiègne, and Paris would then be within easy reach.

But again their plans were doomed to failure. Fighting stubbornly every inch of the way, the French 7th and 11th Corps were pushed back to the line formed by the Savieres stream and running through the villages of Dammard, Bussiares and Etrépilly during the 1st of June. On the same day the line to the north was pushed back to the villages of Longpont,

Missy-aux-Bois, Ambleny and Autrêches, but only after terrific fighting and terrible losses had been inflicted upon the Germans.

During the 2nd of June, the brunt of their attack was concentrated on the territory to the south of Villers-Cottêrets forest. Here the fighting was intense all day long and it fell to the French 2nd Cavalry Corps, who arrived on the scene late in the day, to finally turn the tide and establish a firm base of defense between the towns of Dammard and Veuilly.

The night of June 2nd was again fairly active. Our division, the 20th, supported by some units of the 7th U. S. Infantry, which had taken over a portion of the line near Courthiézy, made a brilliant counterattack and succeeded in driving the Boche back across the river. The casualties from this party did not begin to trickle in until the morning of the 3rd. As the American cars were found to be too heavy and cumbersome to make the difficult trip down the valley from Crèzency, our section found itself designated to the job of evacuating the valley. We carried the wounded out of the valley as far as Condé where they were transferred to the larger American cars for transportation back into the interior. We didn't exactly relish this arrangement because the road down the valley was not the most healthy place in the world to travel over. Due to this arrangement, I carried my first load of American wounded. The boys seemed to take it splendidly; there was little yelling and very few complaints. It would appear from what we are able to hear that the majority of American casualties would be avoided if the boys would realize that the best thing to do is to dig in wherever possible. But it seems that their pride prevents them from taking advantage of what little safety is afforded by this method of protection. Like all new troops, they scoff at danger and continue to expose themselves to useless hazards. The French shrug their shoulders at these evidences of useless bravado and realize that they will soon learn from costly experience that only the living remain to fight. As one Frenchman said, "A live man in a shell hole is worth a hundred dead corps strewn across a field."

June the 3rd again brought a massed attack of terrific intensity along the Villers-Cottêrets front. But again the French managed to stem the tide and hold the front at virtually the same points that they had established the previous evening. From that day on, June 3rd, it was evident that the Germans had exhausted their efforts and, although the fight continued to be active in many places along the line, the assaults were less fierce and had neither the strategic importance nor the intensity of the preceding days. The Crown Prince's army, composed of 34 divisions of the very finest German troops, had been stopped. It is true that they had captured more territory by direct assault then had been gained in all the previous long years of fighting. It is also true that they had captured 63,000 prisoners and great quantities of guns and ammunition. But they had been stopped. The realization of that fact had a tremendous psychological effect on us all. Somehow or other we all expressed again that old feeling of the certainty of ultimate victory. Sometime, probably not so far off, we would end this thing and return to sanity.

Things quieted down near daybreak and most of the cars were sent back to Baulne to get some rest. I had just finished refueling my car when Wholey came up with the unwelcome message that the Medicine Chef wanted a car and had asked for me. So, after getting a bit to eat, I started out. I picked the old boy up at Péroy and returning took an obscure road over the plateau to the little town of Nestles, just south of Château-Thierry. He had some business to transact with the G.B.D. of the 33rd Colonials, who were defending the town with the assistance of the 7th M.G. Corps of the 3rd American Division. While awaiting the return of the Major, I tried to get some idea of what had happened around Château-Thierry during the last few days.

Un soldat mort.

Briefly, this is the story. Realizing that the Germans could not be kept out of the northern portion of the town, the French, on the night of June 1st, had prepared to trap the Boche at the main bridge. The bridge had been mined and the Americans and French Colonials had been placed in ambush in the houses on the southern bank. When the Boche were well across, it was planned to blow up the bridge and then methodically cut them down, caught like rats between the ambush and the river's edge.

But something went wrong. The bridge was blown up too soon with the result that it was the rear guard units of the French and Americans who were caught on the other side of the river. Most of these units managed to effect a crossing at the railroad bridge to the west of the town, but many of the men, including about fifty Senegalese, in trying to swim the river to safety, were shot down by the Americans who thought their cries were German

French Colonial Adjutant and troops.

shouts of victory. But regardless of the result of this unfortunate occurrence, the French were universally loud in their praise of the valiant action of the Americans in preventing the Germans from gaining a foothold on the southern bank of the river.

It was on this trip that I heard firsthand the true facts about the defense of Château-Thierry. The southern push of the Germans in the Château-Thierry sector had really been stopped by the French during the days of May 31st and June 1st. To the left of the town, where the river turns south, on a line with the villages of Torcy, Belleau, Bouresches and Vaux, the dismounted French Cavalry Corps, the 2nd, had borne the brunt of the fighting. The 10th and the 33rd French Colonials had held the town of Château-Thierry and the important Hill 204 to its immediate left.

During the evening of May 31st, a few units of the 7th M.G. Corps of the 3rd American Division had arrived and were immediately sent to the support of the French 10th Colonials. They did magnificent work in the defense of the town of Château-Thierry and the village of Vaux, at the foot of Hill 204. But it was French troops that had really stopped the Germans.

During the first few days of June other units of the American 3rd Division came up to reinforce the French to the right of Château-Thierry, and it was not until June 2nd that the first units of the American 2nd Division arrived to reinforce the French to the left of the village. It is to this famous American Division, the 2nd, that popular history generally accords the palm for stopping the Germans at this famous battle. As a matter of fact, the Germans had been stopped and the line had been well consolidated by the time the first of the famous Marines arrived on the scene. Furthermore, this objective had been accomplished with comparatively little loss in killed and wounded. The famous battle for the control of the Bois Belleau was from a strategic standpoint one of the most useless and costly operations in the annals of history. Instead of being among the bright spots of American history, the affair should be recorded as one of the most flagrant examples of American stupidity, a costly gesture that was to demand the lives of over 9,000 American boys in killed and wounded. Here is the story:

The Bois Belleau lay about 10 kilometers to the west of Château-Thierry and south on a narrow gauge railroad. Being of no strategic importance, the French had abandoned it willingly during the fighting of May 31st, and had established their line along a knoll to the south of the woods. When the 2nd American Division arrived on the scene during the evening of the 2nd of June, the Germans were well entrenched on the southern side of the woods and soon had established an elaborate system of machine gun nests in the middle of the woods and along its upper end. The woods had become a virtual fortress.

It has definitely been established that the French command did not suggest operations against this point. In fact, the American command was requested time after time to give up its useless and costly attempt to gain this position of no strategic use. But after the first few attempts to gain a foothold in the woods had proven to no avail, the American command become more and more stubborn, finally requesting a free hand in attaining their objective. So, day after day, week after week, wave after wave of Americans were sent forward to the slaughter. Regardless of French counsel to desist, the American command held stubbornly to its test. Finally, the two Marine regiments, the 5th and the 6th, which together with the 9th and the 23rd Regiments of regulars made up the 2nd Division, had become so decimated that a regiment of the 3rd Division had to be called to relieve them. On the 15th of June they gained a foothold in the woods, only to be driven out on the succeeding day. So the carnage continued, and as the losses began to pile up the stubbornness of the American command became more evident. It was not until the 25th of June, some 23 days after they had first begun the attack, that the woods were finally taken. An all-day concentration of artillery on the woods had preceded the attack of the 3rd Battalion of the 5th Marines, who finally succeeded in sweeping to the northern edge of the wood, taking 300 German prisoners and some 20-odd machine guns.

The Americans had achieved their first major victory, but at a cost of 9,000 killed and wounded and a fabulous expenditure of shells and ammunition. But the honor of the American command had been vindicated. One can imagine the pride with which Generals Bundy, Harbord and Lewis reported their achievement to the H.Q. at Chaumont. In the papers at home their names were emblazoned across the newspapers as national heroes. The French officially recognized the action by a citation in the orders of the day, to quote: "Thanks to the bravery, fighting spirit and tenacity of the men, who stoically bore fatigue and losses, thanks to the activity and energy of the officers as also to the personal influence of its commander, General J. Harbord, the efforts of the 4th Brigade were entirely successful." At a cost of a mere 9,000 men, a wood is captured, an American General's criminal stubbornness is vindicated and, acclaimed a national hero, he is awarded a Croix de Guerre.

I was back at the section at about 5:00 on the afternoon of June 3rd.

June 2nd, 1918

My Dear Mother,

This is the first time I have had the opportunity of writing in a long, long time. We have been working continuously, sometimes going without food or sleep, for days at a time. We are out of communication with the interior and have not been able to send or receive letters. It is because I had an extra long run back into the country that I was able to get this off. I realize you have had cause to worry, but I bid you not to. I am well but extremely worn out. We have all been fortunate. The section is doing fine. We have as yet failed to evacuate all the *blessés* before the posts were moved back. I hope it will soon be over.

> With love,
> Royce.

August 4th, 1918

My Dear Mother,

I realize it has been a long time since I last wrote and I am heartily ashamed of the fact. My action is more unforgivable because I realize that you have probably worried. But as this is the first time and as I am just a wee bit justified, I hope you will forgive my selfishness in not writing, and I furthermore promise to never let another week go by without writing.

The only excuse I have to offer is that I have really been through too much this summer to do anything but work and rest when I have had the chance. I have been lucky or unlucky to be with divisions which have born the brunt of the three main German offensives. How I even came out unscratched is beyond me, but suffice to say, I am safe and sound. From the middle of May to the present moment it has been one long nightmare. I have written not a soul. No time, inclinations or ambition. And we are going up again in a few days. For times we have lost all communication with the outer world. My hopes of forgiveness are based on these preceding facts.

The fellows in the new section are a fine lot of lads. Four are from Rochester, N.Y., and it may be possible that you will be able to meet their parents. Phil Robeson (father Robeson cutlery works), Mort Miller (father insurance business), Hogy Brown and Lambert Drum.

The section has been doing fine work of late and we expect a citation. Our lieutenant and one man were wounded, another gassed in the last fray.

Yours lovingly,

Royce

P.S. I hope to have good news for you later.

August 9th, 1918

My Dear Mother,

Working rather hard yesterday so could not write. Was awakened in the morning by an intense barrage fire and it was not long before we got orders to send all cars out. The Boche threw gas shells over for a period of three hours, and as the day was still damp and foggy, it worked havoc with our regiment. All cars worked from six in the morning to ten that night carrying gas cases— mustard gas, which burns the sensitive parts of the body. All cases were made to take baths and put on new clothes. A large number will probably be blind as a result.

Got back from my last trip feeling rather low. Reported to doctor who said I had a slight touch of gas. My nostrils are very inflamed and my eyes and throat are affected slightly. Feel much better this morning. Mathew, Rick and Fred Baldwin left on permission today. My turn comes soon. They are going to Paris first and will probably end up at Aix-les-Bains. Dicky is going to send a cable to you for me. Hope so to relieve your worrying. Mail service is very poor of late—haven't received letters in quite a while.

Hoping you are all tip-top and with lots of love,

Your son,

Royce

P.S. See if you can't send me some Spaulding underwear through Canada.

August 18th, 1918

Dear Folks,

Just a note to let you know that I am still serving time in good health. Nothing much to write about. We are again in the lines and life has resumed its same old monotonous run. But the sector is much more dangerous then before. The Boche, in their last party, took such position that they command a view of all our sector making all movements in the daytime very dangerous. As fires of any sort would immediately betray the dugouts, the food has to be prepared behind the lines and sent up. Nothing reaches the lines more than lukewarm and it is, therefore, very hard on the men.

The other day while at ---- I witnessed a very spectacular proceeding. Something like 50 different regiments were decorated and a parade followed the ceremony. It was very impressive to see the long line of men with the battle-scarred flags go swinging along to the

Parade at Cathédrale Notre Dame, Rheims.

enthusiastic applause of the French civilians. Each detachment brought forth its share of "bravos," but the American flag, carried by a detachment of American colored troops who had undergone the worst of the fighting in the last party, cheered ---- all others. Just a little illustration of how the French appreciate our efforts over here.

Yesterday we heard the best news. Our section (643) has received the highest honor conferrable. We have been cited in the orders of the day of our army, which means a Croix de Guerre with a palm, the highest degree of the French war cross. You can imagine how pleased we are to have this honor conferred upon us. This is the second citation the section has received. I will send a copy home for you to see.

Well, I must leave you now, assuring you that I am in the best of health and ever thinking of you at home.

Royce

P.S. I expect to go on another permission very soon. I would be very thankful for some summer underwear.

Lettre de Félicitations.

To Whom it may Concern:

        This is to certify that the bearer, Private Wolfe, Avery R., 10254, of S.S.U. 653, USAAS, with the French Army, is fully entitled and authorized to wear the following decorations:

        CROIX DE GUERRE WITH SILVER STAR.
        AMERICAN FIELD SERVICE MEDAL.

Signed: *W. L. Peebles*

W. L. Peebles, 1st Lt. USAAS.
Commanding.

CARTE d'IDENTITÉ

donnant droit à tous les avantages de

L'ASSOCIATION NATIONALE
DES CROIX DE GUERRE

Signature du Titulaire :

PHOTO

Légalisation du Maire ou
du Commissaire de Police

Fait à

le

ASSOCIATION NATIONALE DES CROIX DE GUERRE

SIÈGE SOCIAL :
4, Boulevard des Invalides, PARIS (VII⁰)

Groupe de : *Amerique*

N° d'ordre général *372*

N° d'ordre au groupe

Mⁿ Avery Royce Wolfe 120 Broadway R. 3705 New York 5 N.Y. USA

MEMBRE *Allié*

Le Trésorier général :

Le Président général :

A.R. Wolfe is awarded the Croix de Guerre.

Epilogue

Final Letters

24 Aout 1918

My Dear Mother,

Quite unexpectedly I was permitted to go on permission. I have just arrived in Paris where I expect to spend a few days. O'Brien, our top sergeant, is with me and we expect to have quite a pleasant furlough. He is an older man than myself, about thirty-eight, and he was in the coal business at Salt Lake City before coming over. It has been unusually hot the last few days but we were lucky in having it rain this morning, so our five hour trip to Paris was not so uncomfortable as it might have been.

Everybody here is enthusiastic over the brilliant success of our troops. After the last *fracas* things have been rather quiet in our sector but we hope to see some more action soon.

I think I told you that the section has won a Croix de Guerre with a palm. We are all very proud to receive this distinction but I wouldn't want to go through what we did again to win another palm.

The mail has been very tardy of late but I hope there will be lots of letters from you waiting for me when I rejoin the section. Any others don't count as you are the only person I am writing to now. I hope Milton keeps his head and doesn't get into this thing until he has to. This life would ruin anybody.

With love to Father, Spencer, Milt and you especially, I remain your son,
Royce

August 28th, 1918

My Dear Mother,
Still in Paris but expect to pull out tomorrow night. Have met quite a number of old friends, and am incidentally having a good time. Hope if I cable for a little gold it will not be inconvenient for you to send it. Costs quite a little to live over here.

Love to all, your loving son,
Royce

January 2nd, 1919

My Dear Mother,

Have been at Nice for the last two days. Menton was a bit dead so I ran down here to see the New Year in. Quite a success. Plan to go back to Menton tonight and leave for section Saturday. Met Milt Potter yesterday and through him learned a lot of news from Buffalo. He is certainly leading a hard life in this war. A softy job in a base hospital miles behind the line, a two month permission home and then, after a month, another permission of two weeks at Nice. I wish I had been wise and joined something like that.

It is very wonderful down here. The only thing that I have against it is that there is too much scenery that greets you at every turn of the head. The promenade on New Year's afternoon was a remarkable sight. French women certainly know how to dress. Had picture taken and will send same at earliest opportunity. Hope I find some money waiting for me at the section because I am terribly low. There is a good rumor afloat that we are posting February. I hope it's true.

Love to all,
Royce

January 20th, 1919

My Dear Mother,

We have moved to Mézières where we are rather comfortably installed in a private residence. Some time ago we lost our division, and since then not a car has moved. We do nothing but wait patiently for the time when we will be able to go home.

There are no definite rumors about this and no one seems to think that we will get home within the next four or five months. It all seems so utterly foolish. Here we are, not doing a thing, using up the country's money when we really should be back there with you. I have become so discouraged that I am seriously contemplating joining the Red Cross. This would mean another six months over here, but at least would get an immediate discharge from the army.

I think you will see my point in this matter and I hope that you will not have any serious objections if I decide to act upon my preset plans concerning the Red Cross.

There is so little of interest in this life that nothing comes from my effort to make this letter interesting. So, longing to get home and with love to you all, I will leave you.

Ever your loving son,

Royce

February 17th, 1919

We have stopped at this town for the night on the way to Aix-la-Chappelle. This will give me a chance to see Germany. In good health,

Royce

Grevenbroich, Germany – February 21st, 1919

My Dear Mother,

We arrived in this town the day before yesterday, three days out from Brussels. You will find it half-way between Aix-la-Chappelle (Aachen) and Düsseldorf. We are attached to the 77th French Division which is occupying this territory. Although this trip has delayed my homecoming to some extent, I think the experience is worth the delay. I find that with the exception of a few luxuries, Germany has been little affected by the war. Of course, a number of families have lost a son or a father and there has been what we call "hard times" for a year or so, but the country itself is intact and the population has not been compelled to realize the frightfulness of the war as the people of the invaded countries have.

The country is thickly dotted with factories which are still functioning perfectly. The life in the cities is as normal as ever, streetcar service, electric lights, railroad service, all continuing as before. Compare the state of prosperity with the devastated portions of France and Belgium. The Boche have really gained a victory. They have practically succeeded in their pre-war policy of crippling France industrially, while she is ready at this moment to flood the world with cheap articles of export. She has taken from the occupied regions everything of value, machinery, articles of art value, has ravaged the French coal mines, and she in turn has gone untouched.

Believe me, she has got to pay for all this and pay heavily. But I fear that she will get off lightly. If she does it will be a crime.

We hear rumors that we are to leave for Sille on the 25th of this month. This looks very encouraging as in all probability we will go from there to the base camp near Paris. This is the starting point for home.

We have not received much mail since we left Mézières over two weeks ago, but it ought to be coming along soon.

With love to you all and hoping to hear from you soon,

Royce

February 27th, 1919

Dear Mother,

Last night we were in Germany, tonight we are in Belgium, and tomorrow night we will be in France. Who knows but that a few weeks will find me home.

Lovingly,

Royce

March 13th, 1919

Dear Mother,

I know you will be glad to learn that I ought to be home within six weeks at the most. Our section has arrived in a staging area and it is expected that we will leave for the port of embarkation by the last of the month.

Life down here is surely military, the first real touch of intensive camp life that I have come in contact with. There are some 500 men in the camp. We get up at seven in the morning and are kept busy until five at night with the numerous details. Tomorrow the section is going into quarantine in preparation for leaving. All troops going home are thoroughly deloused and disinfected before leaving.

I have met many old acquaintances here, among them Lieutenant Bolton, Sandy's brother. He left yesterday, very anxious to get back because of his engagement to Beatrice Holmes. I also ran across Margerie Whitbeck's brother.

We are all terribly put out because of the order which takes ten men from our section. All chaps who had not suited by January 1st, 1918 are to be sent back to the front. This is very disappointing as the boys had written home that they would be home soon. Lieutenant B---, who I have known for a long time, Lafayette man, gave me the letter which Dad wrote about my discharge. He asked me to explain that he could do nothing that would get me home any sooner.

An order has come out within the last few days which enables us old Field Servicemen to be immediately discharged here in France. After considering the matter, I have decided that such a step would be needlessly expensive and I might just as well go home "on the government." Nothing much to say but that this is practically sure dope six weeks or even four weeks will see me back.

Yours as ever,
Royce.

April 1st, 1919

Dear Folks,

Most discouraging news. We are being held up at Brest indefinitely—a hell of a hole and we are living a terrible life. Don't know when we will be sent home. If I only had funds for passage home I could get out over there. As it is, I am working awfully hard for any passage home if I ever get any.

In the best of spirits,
Royce

Returning home.

Afterword

More than 4 million men died on the Western Front in the First World War out of a total of 15 million casualties suffered by both Allies and the Central Powers. One out of every six men who served in the war was a fatality.

The Versailles Convention met in Paris in January 1919, barely two months after the general armistice declared on November 11, 1918. The Treaty of Versailles would prove to be only a temporary truce that endured barely a generation prior to the Second World War.

Avery Royce Wolfe returned to the United States in May 1919, almost two years after his departure to join the voluntary ambulance service. He had enlisted "for the duration" of the conflict. On his discharge in May 1919 he returned to the United States and completed his course in mechanical engineering at Lafayette College. He married Florence Braithwaite, a book publishing editor in New York. The couple never had children. Wolfe would continue his personal journals for the rest of his life. After a long and successful career in the mining industry he died from cancer in Tucson, Arizona in 1977. He left an enduring legacy of service to his country.

Enlistment and discharge papers

Glossary of Terms

Annamite: native of French-Indochina, now Vietnam

abri: dugout

ambuscade: ambush

arrivé: in-coming (as an artillery shell)

assis: seated, slightly wounded soldier

au revoir: good-bye

avant la guerre: pre-war

avion: airplane

beaucoup: much, many

beaucoup d'étoiles et une grande lune: many stars and a full moon

bidon: kettle, canteen or tin used to carry gasoline, water or oil on a car

blessés: wounded

Boche: derogatory term for German, probably from French alboche—cabbage

bon compagnon: companion

brancardier: stretcher bearer

briquet: gas stove, lighter

camion: truck

camionette: small truck

c'est bien: that's good

cave voûtée: vaulted cellar

c'est la guerre: it's the war, it can't be helped

chef: chief or supervisor, the American officer in command of a volunteer ambulance section

Cheval Blanc: White Horse

claxon: alarm

couché: lain down, a stretcher-case, a severely wounded soldier

couchez: lying down v.

coup de main: surprise attack in order to take prisoners for interrogation

cuisinier: cook

curé: priest

demi-tour a droit: half-turn to the right
D.S.A.: Direction des Services Automobile (French Motor Transport)
départ: out-going (as an artillery shell)
Desperate Desmond: character from early 20c. strip cartoon
deux: two
doucement: gently

éclat: burst (as of shrapnel)
en avant marche: march on!
en ligne: in line!
en panne: broken down (as a vehicle)
en repos: resting
essence: gasoline
état-major: general staff

face à gauche: turn left
fourragère: a military decoration awarded to an entire unit, worn as a braided cord
gare: station
gendarme: policeman
grave: serious
grave blessé: gravely wounded
guardez-vous: be careful
guerre: war
guerre mondiale: world war

H.O.E.: Hospital Of Evacuation
hôpital de triage: triage or sorting hospital

Kronprinz: Crown Prince
le Galle: scabies
Le Mort Homme: The Dead Man—name of a hill near Verdun

maréchal de logis: chief of supply
mari: town hall
mort: dead

parc: park
petite: small
pinard/penard: cheap wine
piste: track
Place de la Gare: railroad square
poilu: a French soldier
poste de secour: aid station

quinze: fifteen

ravitaillement wagon: field kitchen
rompez vos rangs: break ranks, dismissed

S.O.L.: out of luck, unfortunate, "shit out of luck"
S.S.U.: Section Sanitaire (États) Unis American Ambulance Section
sabot: wooden shoe, clog
soixante-quinze: 75 (as in 75 mm howitzer)
sous-chef: under chief or lieutenant

tout de suite: quickly
triage: see hôpital de triage
trois: three

un peu d'essence: a little gasoline
une: one

voiture: coach

Zouave: soldier of French infantry corps created in Algeria in 1831

Bibliography and Reference Material

Ayres, Leonard P. *The War With Germany: A Statistical Summary* (Washington, 1919).

William L. Foley Collection, *American Volunteer Ambulance Drivers in World War I: 1914–1918* (Hamden, CT, 2007).

Hansen, Arlen J. *Gentlemen Volunteers: The Story of the American Ambulance Drivers in the Great War, August 1914–September 1918* (New York: Arcadia Publishing, 1996).

Hart, B.H. Liddell, *The War in Outline: 1914–19* (New York: Random House, 1936).

History of the American Field Service in France, as Told by Its Members (New York: Houghton Mifflin, 1920)

Heyman Neil M., *Daily Life in World War One* (Westport, CT).

Shermer, David. *World War I* (Secaucus, NJ: Derby Books, 1975).

Smucker, John R. Jr. *The History of the United States Army Ambulance Service, 1917–1918–1919* (United States Army Ambulance Service Association, 1967).

Tuchman, Barbara W. *The Guns of August* (New York: Dell Publishing Co., 1962).

Tuchman, Barbara W. *The Proud Tower* (New York: Macmillan, 1966).